The Divine Pattern

by

Adrian Ebens

ASPECT Books

www.ASPECTBooks.com

The Divine Pattern

Copyright © 2012 Adrian Ebens

ISBN-13: 978-1-57258-748-9

Library of Congress Control Number: 2011946130

Book Website
www.divine-pattern.com
Email: adrian@maranathamedia.com

Unless otherwise stated, all Bible references
are taken from the King James Bible.

Published by
ASPECT Books
www.ASPECTBooks.com

In memory of James White
A man of gospel order

Thank you...

A special note of thanks to all those from the Maranatha Media online community who contributed in some way or another to getting this book together. I would just like to thank a number of people, who our Father has placed a desire in my heart to bless.

To Rachel and Curly. Thank you so much for taking the time to get involved and support this project. May our Father bless your family abundantly.

To Mark, Bonnie and the *In the Heavens* Online Forum. Thanks for your kind and generous feedback. May the sweetness of Jesus be always with you.

Thank you Joanne and Susan for your checking and rechecking things. You both have been "a mother in Israel" in these sad times. May our Father bless you with peace and grant you the desires of your heart.

To Cristina and Jenni. Thank you for remembering our son Daniel. You have blessed us through your kindness. May our Father reward you with everlasting peace and joy.

To Graham and Harmina. Your prayers and support have been a blessing from heaven. May our Father bless you with joy in His Son.

To my brother Michael. Your passion for this message has really blessed me. May your passion flow to many others.

To my brother Frank. Your suggestions and feedback have really helped expand and edify this work. May our Father bless you and all that come within your sphere of influence.

To my brother Corey. Thank you for demonstrating the principles in this book so faithfully. May your tribe increase.

To Gary and Carolyn. Lorelle and I can't express how much of a blessing you have been to us.

To my mother and father who have stood by me through these tough times. Your love and support have been a source of strength and much needed encouragement.

To my beloved Lorelle who has stood my side and walked this narrow path with me. I could never have produced this work without you. May all the daughters of Zion rise up and call you blessed.

Contents

Section 1. Foundations of the Divine Pattern

1. The Divine Pattern

> **1 Cor 8:6** But to us there is but one God, the Father, **of whom**[1] are all things, and we in him; and one Lord Jesus Christ, **by whom** are all things, and we by him.

Everything we receive in this life comes to us through the divine pattern. This pattern is revealed to us by the persons of the Father and the Son. This divine pattern finds its source with the Father "Of whom are all things" and then is passed onto us through the person of Christ "By whom are all things."

It is vitally important for us as the recipients of these blessings to clearly discern the personality and individuality of each person in this divine pattern.

> **Heb 1:1-3** God, who at sundry times and in divers manners spake in time past unto the fathers by the prophets, (2) Hath in these last days spoken unto us by his Son, whom he hath appointed heir of all things, by whom also he made the worlds; (3) Who being the brightness of his glory, and the express image of his person, and upholding all things by the word of his power, when he had by himself purged our sins, sat down on the right hand of the Majesty on high;

> **John 5:26** For as the Father hath life in himself; so hath he given to the Son to have life in himself;

---

[1] All bold emphasis within quotes throughout this book have been supplied.

1

The Divine Pattern

The Bible clearly reveals the Father as the great source of all and that His Son is His express image and received all things from Him. Since the Son has received all things from His Father and is His express image, the only way we can mentally tell them apart is that the Son came from the Father and inherited all things from Him. His inheritance is the secret to preserving the personality and individuality of each. His inheritance also makes clear and distinct the "Of Whom" and "By Whom" sequence of the divine pattern.

As we read through Scripture we can find several examples where the "Of Whom" and "By Whom" pattern is replicated. Some of these examples overlap because of the cascading nature of God's blessings flowing through several vessels.

Source – Of Whom	Channel – By Whom	References
Father	Son	1 Cor 8:6; 1 Cor 11:3; Heb 1:1-3
Husband	Wife	Gen 3:16; 1 Cor 11:3; Eph 5:25; 1 Pet 3:1
Father	Mother	Ex 20:12; Eph 6:1; Col 3:20
Mother	Children	1 Tim 2:15
Christ	Husband	1 Cor 11:3
Christ	Church	Eph 5:25
Prophet	Priest	Ex 4:16; Lev 8:36
Elder/Pastors	Flock	1 Pet 5:2; 1 Thess 5:12,13
King/ Governor	Subjects/ Citizens	Rom 13:1-3; 1 Pet 2:13,14
Bible	Spirit of Prophecy	RH Jan 20, 1903 "Lesser Light"
Bible	Pastor/Elder	2 Tim 4:2; 1 Pet 5:2

The more fully this divine pattern is followed the more blessings will flow upon us and our families. For instance when we honour our father and mother, we are promised long life. When we esteem highly in love those who are over us, we are blessed by their preaching of the Word and exhortations to a godly life.

The Divine Pattern

Apart from the direct blessings of joy, happiness and fellowship that flow to us through this divine pattern, there are also the protective blessings that we can accrue through the channel. In each case, the one "By Whom" things come, is under the protection and possesses the authority of the one "Of Whom" things come.

As an example of how much protection a child can have, we see:

1. The child is protected by the mother,
2. Who is protected by her husband,
3. Who is protected by the police,
4. Who are protected by the government,
5. Which is ordained of God.

Taking this in a spiritual direction we see:

1. The father is exhorted by the elders or pastor,
2. Who are subject to the Word of God,
3. Which was written by the prophets,
4. Which was and is given by Christ,
5. Who receives it from His Father.

The more we move into positions reflecting the divine pattern the greater our protection, blessing, peace and joy. The key principle of the Father's plan is that:

1. All things are received through a channel and not directly from the Father.
2. All things are patterned on the Father and His Son.

The rebellion of Satan introduced concepts that marred this divine pattern. The order of Heaven meant that originally Lucifer was under the authority of Christ, who was under the authority of His Father.

> Satan, the chief of the fallen angels, once had an exalted position in Heaven. He was next in honor to Christ. *Review and Herald*, Feb 24, 1874.

The Scripture tells us how Satan wished to alter the divine pattern:

> **Isa 14:12-14** How art thou fallen from heaven, O Lucifer, son of the morning! how art thou cut down to the ground, which didst weaken the nations! (13) For thou hast said

> in thine heart, I will ascend into heaven, I will exalt my
> throne above the stars of God: I will sit also upon the
> mount of the congregation, in the sides of the north: (14)
> I will ascend above the heights of the clouds; I will be like
> the most High.

In these texts we see a being who does not seek to be under the protection and care of the divine pattern but rather seeks to be like, meaning to resemble, the Most High. Originally this meant that Satan wanted to be made equal to Christ rather than be under His authority, so that he could report directly to the Father without being under Christ. The Father, via the divine pattern, moved to defend and protect His Son and declared the relationship that He sustained to all the creation. Christ did not defend Himself or speak in His own defence. All this was done by the Father. Satan rejected the Father's command to worship and honour His Son and then desired to be exactly like the Most High.

Our worship of God is based only upon our reading of the Word of God. Our knowledge of Him comes to us through what He has revealed to us in His Word and by what He has created. Our understanding of who God is and our worship of Him while we live in this sinful world only occur in the mind. If we deviate from the explicit statements of Scripture our minds will immediately fall into idolatry. This is Satan's objective, to cause us to go beyond the Word in order to perceive God in our minds as some form other than the divine pattern. Thus he takes from us the hedge of protection and gains more access to control, possess and destroy us.

Notice carefully that Satan desired to be the same as the Most High. Through a cunning process Satan has deceived the Christian world into making Christ exactly the same as the Father. As the Christian world worships God through its various creeds, the entity perceived as the second person of the Godhead is actually a formulation of Satan.[2] By presenting Christ as exactly the same as the Father in every way, Satan confuses the human mind through the law of indiscernibility,

---

[2] "Satan is not only demonstrating the immortality of the soul by spirit manifestations, but as in the beginning he taught plurality of gods…Spiritualism could effect little had not the way been prepared by the false teachings of those who profess to believe the Bible. Satan foresaw this, and has managed to get the fundamental articles of his creed into the creeds of all the popular churches." R.F. Cottrell, *Review and Herald*, Apr 14, 1859.

meaning that two things possess the exact same qualities so that they no longer can be clearly discerned separately, they become mysteriously one through their loss of individuality.

The central aim of Satan's strategy to strip away our blessing and protection is to cause a corruption in our minds concerning the divine pattern. He seeks to seduce us by granting to the one "By Whom" the same attributes as the one "Of Whom." We are seduced by what appears to be a desire to exalt the person in the channel, but the opposite occurs. As the one who was originally "By Whom" becomes more and more like the one "Of Whom" the less we are able to discern the difference, until the only thing left is two or even three "Of Whoms." That causes reason to collapse, thus opening the door to the mystical. As we shall learn later, this simple little process is the secret of the abominating desolator.

There is plenty of evidence to show where this warping and twisting has occurred to the divine pattern. Take the following examples:

Catholicism

Catholicism took the words of the priest and made them equal to the word of the prophets contained in the Bible. Through this process the word of the Roman pontiff completely superseded the Scriptures. Here is one example:

> The Pope has power to change times, to abrogate laws
> and to dispense with all things, even the precepts of
> Christ. - *Decretal De Translat. Espiscop. Cap*

Protestantism

As a reaction to this perversion, Protestantism restored the Word as the sole authority for the conscience, but Satan then manages to pervert this process by taking away any authority from the pastors or leaders of the church. Each man reads the Bible for himself, which is correct, but then each man feels at complete liberty to rebuke and overturn the position of leaders whenever he chooses. Satan does not care which direction you go as long as you miss the divine pattern of "Of Whom" and "By Whom." The net effect of Protestantism is to split and divide, split and divide and become vulnerable to every wind of doctrine and every rising of charismatic leadership.

The above examples reveal the perversion of the prophet/priest image of the divine pattern. Let's take this to another level where the male/female image is twisted regarding the priesthood or ministry.

Priesthood

Once again Satan has moved Catholicism one way and Protestantism the other. Satan moved the Catholic Church to give male priests absolute power and control, causing untold misery and sorrow for women. He then moves within Protestant churches through a positive desire to lift the role of women and gives them a voice in the church by granting them the same position as elders and pastors. This causes an accelerated cascade effect on the perception of marital equality, causing the mind to merge the two parts of the divine pattern into one and pressing male and female entities towards a unisex mindset.

As each reflection of the divine pattern becomes confused and mystified, the "By Whom" elements move out from under the protection of their "Of Whom" counterpart, being liberated by "enlightened co-equality." Satan then can move in and harm our children, our wives, our churches, our pastors, our governments and our world.

An observation of western society should tell us that every aspect of the divine pattern has been marred and therefore all levels of protection have been severely penetrated by the wicked one.

The natural Adventist response to seeing truth perverted is to take the Protestant approach and take the sword to the leaders of the church and blame them for the degradation. Satan is content for this work to occur, he knows it still breaks the divine pattern and will keep churches from being blessed.

In a later chapter I will address aspects of what to do when the divine pattern is completely marred in the church and what process we need to go through to restore the channel of blessing and reclaim the divine pattern. But next I want to show you the divine pattern in the Law of God.

2. The Fountain in the Law

In the previous chapter we explored the divine pattern revealed in 1 Corinthians 8:6 speaking of the relationship of the Father and Son. Their relationship itself reveals this divine pattern. It comprises the "Of Whom" Father, who is the source, and the "By Whom" Son, who is the channel.

We cited several examples of how this divine pattern has been replicated in various levels of family, church and community.

One place that this divine pattern is wonderfully revealed is in the Ten Commandments. If we study the law carefully we find that eight of the commandments contain prohibitions while the two commandments at the heart of the law contain a positive blessing. Notice:

> **Gen 2:3** And God **blessed the seventh day**, and sanctified it: because that in it he had rested from all his work which God created and made.

> **Eph 6:2-3** Honour thy father and mother; which is the **first commandment with promise**; (3) That it may be well with thee, and thou mayest live long on the earth.

If we arrange the commandments around these two commandments that have a positive blessing we might see something that resembles a fountain:

The Law as the Fountain of Life

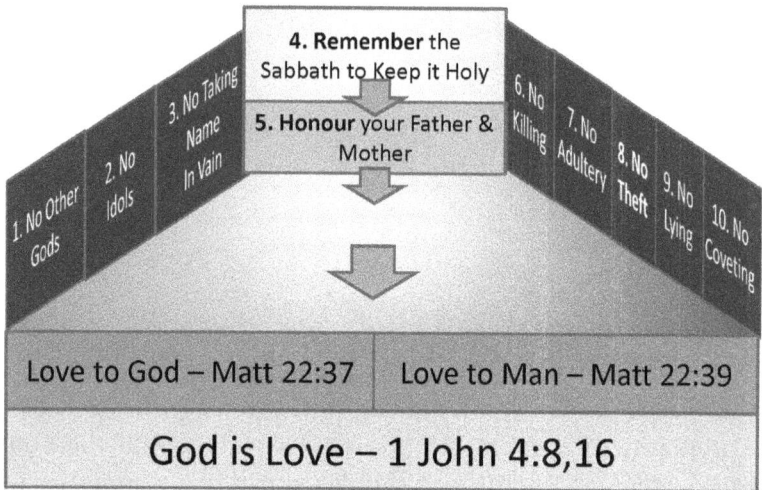

"Of Whom"	"By Whom"
Remember the Sabbath... For in six days the LORD made heaven and earth, the sea, and all that in them is... Ex 20:8-11	Honour Your Father and Mother. Lo, children are an heritage of the LORD: and the fruit of the womb is his reward. Ps 127:3

All the other commandments act as a guardrail to guide us to the source of the fountain found in remembering the Sabbath and honouring our parents. Can we see that the fourth and fifth commandment follow the divine pattern?

God designed that through our parents, we would be taught about the principles of His kingdom, His law and, of course, His love.

> **Deut 6:4-8** Hear, O Israel: The LORD our God is one LORD: (5) And thou shalt love the LORD thy God with all thine heart, and with all thy soul, and with all thy might. (6) And these words, which I command thee this day, shall be in thine heart: (7) **And thou shalt teach them diligently unto thy children**, and shalt talk of them when thou sittest in thine house, and when thou walkest by the way, and when thou liest down, and when thou risest up. (8) And thou shalt bind them for a sign upon thine hand, and they shall be as frontlets between thine eyes.

The Divine Pattern

Is it possible to see that as we approach the law through the divine pattern, the pattern that provides all blessing, we will indeed flourish and be blessed? Please notice carefully what Ellen White says about the fifth commandment:

> This, says the apostle, "is the first commandment with promise." Ephesians 6:2. To Israel, expecting soon to enter Canaan, it was a pledge to the obedient, of long life in that good land; **but it has a wider meaning, including all the Israel of God, and promising eternal life upon the earth when it shall be freed from the curse of sin.** *Patriarchs and Prophets*, page 308.

Ellen White connects the honouring of our parents with having eternal life. How is this possible? When we see that all things come from the Father, the great source of all,[1] and flow through His appointed agencies then we can indeed see that when we honour our parents, we are honouring an authority that God has established.

> "Honor thy father and thy mother: that thy days may be long upon the land which the Lord thy God giveth thee." Parents are entitled to a degree of love and respect which is due to no other person. **God Himself, who has placed upon them a responsibility** for the souls committed to their charge, has ordained that during the earlier years of life, parents shall stand in the place of God to their children. And **he who rejects the rightful authority of his parents is rejecting the authority of God.** *Patriarchs and Prophets*, page 308.

It is through our parents that our Father in Heaven seeks to pour upon us His love, His mercy and His grace. Our parents are a channel through whom our Father wants to bless us with His words of affection and tenderness. This principle is so important that God made His covenant with Abraham dependent on the right ordering of the family after the divine pattern.

> **Gen 18:18-19** Seeing that Abraham shall surely become a great and mighty nation, and all the nations of the earth shall be blessed in him? (19) **For I know him, that he will command his children and his household after him, and**

---

[1] "The Ancient of Days is God the Father. Says the psalmist: "Before the mountains were brought forth, or ever Thou hadst formed the earth and the world, even from everlasting to everlasting, Thou art God." Psalm 90:2. It is He, the source of all being, and the fountain of all law,..." *Great Controversy*, page 479.

they shall keep the way of the LORD, to do justice and judgment; that the LORD may bring upon Abraham that which he hath spoken of him.

God states that He would bring upon Abraham all that He has promised as Abraham commands his family and household after him, meaning that he leads his family to follow the divine pattern where his wife respects him as the head of the house and his children are taught to honour and respect their father and mother. Let us note this carefully:

The covenant was dependent on the right ordering of the family after the divine pattern.

This is why Ellen White states:

> Society is composed of families, and is what the heads of families make it. Out of the heart are "the issues of life"; and the heart of the community, of the church, and of the nation is the household. **The well-being of society, the success of the church, the prosperity of the nation, depend upon home influences**. *Adventist Home*, page 15.

Through those home influences we are meant to learn the divine pattern. As we honour our father and mother as a reflection of the divine pattern of Father and Son, we learn how to connect ourselves to our Father in Heaven. If we disobey our parents and forsake the pattern reflected in our parents we will not be able to connect to the divine pattern in Heaven.

> God designs that the families of earth shall be a symbol of the family in heaven. Christian homes, established and conducted in accordance with God's plan, are among His most effective agencies for the formation of Christian character and for the advancement of His work. *Testimonies, Volume 6*, page 430.

Now I would like you to notice how this divine pattern in the home is extended to the wider community.

> The fifth commandment requires children not only to yield respect, submission, and obedience to their parents, but also to give them love and tenderness, to lighten their cares, to guard their reputation, and to succor and comfort them in old age. **It also enjoins respect for ministers and rulers and for all others to whom God has delegated authority.** *Patriarchs and Prophets*, page 308.

Note carefully that the fifth commandment includes ministers and rulers and all others to whom God has delegated authority. Please underscore this point carefully:

Respect for ministers and rulers is part of the fifth commandment.

There are many voices that cry, "I only need my Bible and I am not under any man!" This is a very cunning ploy of Satan to break the divine pattern. If we truly were not under any man then wives need not respect their husbands and children need not honour their parents. Many people forget that the only reason we have our Bibles is because God instructed the prophets to write down what He desired to be said, and also inspired men to publish and print the Bible.

This cry that "I have my Bible and am not under any man" is a reaction to the work of Satan to move the "By Whom" channel to the same level as the "Of Whom" source. When parents seek to force the conscience of their children in regard to worship they are placing themselves in a position above what God requires. As Ellen White indicated, the fifth commandment also applies to ministers and rulers. When those who fill these positions require of us something contrary to the Word of God, we cannot obey. This does not mean that we also cease to honour or respect them as the "By Whom" channel. We continue to honour them as far as the Word of God requires, no more and no less. As we continue in this book, we will study further how God deals with delegated authorities who assume positions that God alone can occupy. Yet we make the point that an attempt to force our conscience by those granted authority does not grant us the right to completely disregard their authority and break the divine pattern.

When Satan seeks to move an authority figure to merge the "By Whom" channel with the "Of Whom" source, we must remember the admonition of Jesus:

> **Matt 23:9** And call no man your father upon the earth: for one is your Father, which is in heaven.

Yet this counsel does not negate the following:

> **1 Tim 5:1** Rebuke not an elder, but entreat him as a father; and the younger men as brethren;

When our father or church leader seeks our submission in things that alone belong to God, they are merging themselves with God as an authority in our lives and this destroys the personalities of the "Of Whom" and "By Whom" structure. We cannot obey any command that violates this. It is Satan's constant effort to elevate "By Whom" aspects of the channel to the same level as "Of Whom" positions in order to destroy them both.

- He seeks to raise the Son of God to the same level as the Father in order to destroy the Son and the Father.
- He seeks to raise wives to the same position as their husbands in order to destroy their marriage.
- He seeks to raise women to the same position as ordained male pastors, thus confusing the "Of Whom" and "By Whom" pattern of leadership.
- He has sought to raise the writings of Ellen White to the same level as the Bible in order to destroy their distinct roles in guiding us.
- He has sought to raise the words of men to the same level as the Bible by moving leaders to discipline members with the 28 Fundamentals confusing and merging their distinct roles.

Whenever God's people sense that those in authority over them are seeking to require more than their position grants them, Satan then moves those under that authority to completely reject the forceful authority. As the people come out from under that protective authority, Satan is then better positioned to sweep them away with winds of doctrines, false shepherds and potential loss of life.

Let us remember the divine pattern in every aspect of our lives. Just as we behold Christ as a distinct person, holding a distinct authority over us as the ultimate "By Whom" authority, let us remember all the other "By Whom" authorities placed in our lives even when Satan moves them to merge with the "Of Whom" authority above them. Let us not be seduced into rejecting these authorities, but rather plead for them and ask God to bless them and help them regain their true identity and position as a reflection of the divine pattern.

3. The Threefold Cord

> **Eccl 4:12** And if one prevail against him, two shall withstand him; and a threefold cord is not quickly broken.

Any system that is well designed will have a built-in backup if one part of the system fails. The divine pattern that was first given to Adam and Eve as a reflection of Father and Son expanded to the community and the church. Notice what inspiration says:[1]

> At the beginning, the father was constituted [1] priest and [2] magistrate of his own family. Then came the patriarchal rule, which was like that of the family, but extended over a greater number. When Israel became a distinct people, the twelve tribes, springing from the twelve sons of Jacob, had each a leader. These leaders, or elders, were assembled whenever any matter that pertained to the general interest was to be settled. [1] The high priest was the visible representative of Christ, the Redeemer of his people. When the Hebrews settled in Canaan, [2] judges were appointed, who resembled governors. These rulers were invested with authority to declare war and proclaim peace for the nation; but God was still the recognized king of Israel, and he continued to reveal his will to these chosen leaders, and to manifest through them his power. *Signs of the Times*, July 13, 1882.

As the family grew larger, the same "Of Whom" and "By Whom" pattern was replicated in each creating a threefold cord.

---

[1] Numbers in square brackets supplied.

Divine Pattern: Threefold Cord

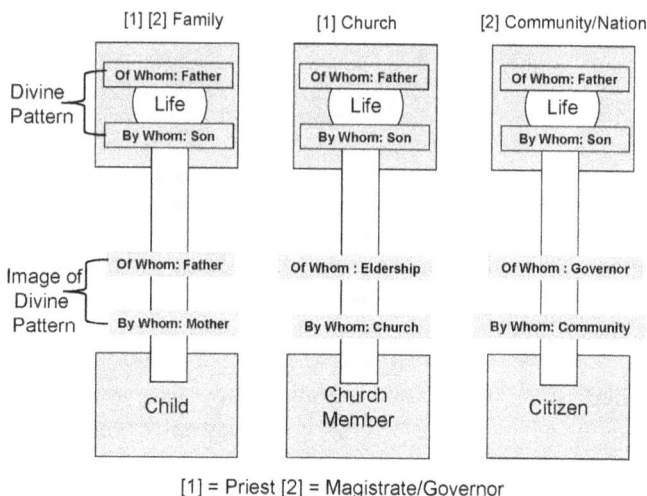

[1] [2] Family	[1] Church	[2] Community/Nation

Divine Pattern

Of Whom: Father	Of Whom: Father	Of Whom: Father
Life	Life	Life
By Whom: Son	By Whom: Son	By Whom: Son

Image of Divine Pattern

Of Whom: Father	Of Whom : Eldership	Of Whom : Governor
By Whom: Mother	By Whom: Church	By Whom: Community

Child	Church Member	Citizen

[1] = Priest [2] = Magistrate/Governor

We notice that while the office of priest and magistrate are the same person in the home, these offices were to be separated in the domain of the wider community, creating a separation of church and state. It is beyond the scope of our present study to detail this separation.

We see the divine pattern in the family clearly expressed by Paul when he stated:

> **1 Cor 11:3** But I would have you know, that the head of every man is Christ; and the head of the woman is the man; and the head of Christ is God.

As we have noted, the church and the community are patterned after the family. Notice again what Ellen White says:

> Society is composed of families, and is what the heads of families make it. Out of the heart are "the issues of life"; and the heart of the community, of the church, and of the nation is the household. The well-being of society, the success of the church, the prosperity of the nation, depend upon home influences. *Adventist Home*, page 15.

The society or community is a subset of both church and nation. Note how Paul connects the pattern of home leadership as a qualification of church leadership:

1 Tim 3:2-5² A bishop then must be blameless, the husband [Of Whom] of one wife [By Whom], vigilant, sober, of good behaviour, given to hospitality, apt to teach; (3) Not given to wine, no striker, not greedy of filthy lucre; but patient, not a brawler, not covetous; (4) One that ruleth well his own house, having his children in subjection [command his children after him Gen 18:19] with all gravity; (5) (For if a man know not how to rule his own house, how shall he take care of the church of God?)

How does the church support a family when the blessing channel in a particular home is broken?

James 1:27 Pure religion and undefiled before God and the Father is this, To visit the fatherless and widows in their affliction, and to keep himself unspotted from the world.

Isa 1:17 Learn to do well; seek judgment, relieve the oppressed, judge the fatherless, plead for the widow.

These passages are addressed to leaders in the church. What is pure religion above all other things? It is to visit the fatherless and the widows in their affliction. Why? Because the home is the strongest reflection of the divine pattern and church leaders need to do all they can to assist families where a father has gone missing either through death or dereliction of duty. When a father was no longer able to bless his children the spiritual leaders of the church were to step in and provide that blessing. This is exactly what Jesus did.

Mark 10:13-16 And they brought young children to him, that he should touch them: and his disciples rebuked those that brought them. (14) But when Jesus saw it, he was much displeased, and said unto them, Suffer the little children to come unto me, and forbid them not: for of such is the kingdom of God. (15) Verily I say unto you, Whosoever shall not receive the kingdom of God as a little child, he shall not enter therein. (16) And he took them up in his arms, put his hands upon them, and blessed them.

Where did the abundance of the blessing that flowed forth from Jesus come from?

Matt 3:17 And lo a voice from heaven, saying, This is my beloved Son, in whom I am well pleased.

---

² Comments in square brackets supplied.

Through Christ the divine pattern went into action and all the promises made to Abraham would be made certain. Abraham was a type of Christ when it was stated to him:

> **Gen 12:2** And I will make of thee a great nation, and I will bless thee, and make thy name great; and thou shalt be a blessing:

It is the Son of God that the Father blessed and made a great nation by Him. Christ stands at the head of this blessing system and pours it through the threefold cord to fill our lives. Notice this process in action:

> **Luke 4:18** The Spirit of the Lord is upon me, because he hath anointed me to preach the gospel to the poor; he hath sent me to heal the brokenhearted, to preach deliverance to the captives, and recovering of sight to the blind, to set at liberty them that are bruised,

> **Matt 28:18-19** And Jesus came and spake unto them, saying, All power is given unto me in heaven and in earth. (19) Go ye therefore, and teach all nations,...

The message of Christ was amongst other things to heal the brokenhearted. What causes a broken heart more than the withering curses of a wretched childhood? For more on the message of Christ see chapter 19 of my book *Life Matters*.[3]

The point we are making here is that the church was designed as a backup system or contingency[4] for families when the "Of Whom" component of the family ceased to function. The community also contributed by ensuring that the fatherless and widows had food and shelter and protection. See Ruth chapter two concerning the practice of gleaning the fields.

When a church and community reflect the divine pattern as an extension of the family, then a child will grow and flourish, and if a family suffers the loss of one of the channels, the other two channels will supply the lack. As the verse says "A threefold cord is not quickly

---

[3] Go to www.life-matters.org

[4] "Christ here gives all His people an example of the manner of His working for the salvation of men. The Son of God identifies Himself with His organized church. His blessings are to come through the agencies He has ordained, and He desires men to connect themselves with this channel of blessing." *Signs of the Times*, November 10, 1898

broken." While this threefold cord is not quickly broken, over time Satan has found ways to break this system.

Satan well knows that the whole channel of blessing rests upon having the divine pattern stamped into our minds. The God we worship is reflected in the home, the church and the community. Satan introduces to mankind an altered pattern; a pattern not of source and channel but of co-equality where the second component is unwittingly merged with the first. This is the secret to the desolation of the family, the church and the community. This is how Satan can break the threefold cord. Once people perceive an inherent co-equality of status in their worship of the divine, then the relationship of marriage is altered to cut the blessing to children; male leadership is neutered in the church and the community and within one generation Satan can take control of the entire community.

There is a direct link between the god that the Church of Rome adores and its ability to desolate the hearts of men. The secret is breaking the divine pattern and replacing it with a version of the three-in-one Trinity. It does not matter what version you adopt as long as you perceive the second person as the same as the first, just with a different title. The Catholic Church does this through a one-substance being and the Adventist Church does it by three different labels for the divine beings that possess identical inherent qualities.

When you perceive that Father and Son are part of a three person yet one-being God, you lose your ability to clearly distinguish one from the other. When you speak of one you are also speaking of the other. Here is how one Trinitarian expressed it:

> There are three persons in the Godhead but they are so mysteriously and indissolubly related to each other that the presence of each one is equivalent to the presence of the others. *W.W Prescott Sermon Notes*, page 8, from Sermon at Takoma Park, Oct 14, 1939.

As you read the following quote, see how long you can keep the Father and Son distinct in your mind:

> We would suggest that God in **His** Trinitarian self-revelation, has claimed that **He** created us to reflect the love that supernaturally resides in **His very being** as an eternally loving God who is one in three. Furthermore, the triune love found in God is not self oriented and

thus strongly implies that we find our greatest joy and satisfaction in living and serving others. Whidden, Moon and Reeve, *The Trinity*, page 247.

The confusion of "Trinitarian self-revelation" was not a part of early Adventist faith. In 1874 the very first issue of the periodical *Signs of the Times*, was edited and published by Elder James White, where 25 Fundamental Principles held "with great unanimity" by the Adventist people were introduced. Here are the principles relating to God. Notice they were modelled on 1 Corinthians 8:6.

1. **That there is one God, a personal, spiritual being**, the creator of all things, omnipotent, omniscient, and eternal, infinite in wisdom, holiness, justice, goodness, truth, and mercy; unchangeable, and everywhere present by his representative, the Holy Spirit. Ps. 139:7.

2. **That there is one Lord Jesus Christ, the Son of the Eternal Father**, the one by whom God created all things, and by whom they do consist; that he took on him the nature of the seed of Abraham for the redemption of our fallen race; . . .

These two statements remained unchanged until 1931[5] , and then in 1980 the mystery of the Trinity was officially voted in as a Fundamental Belief of the Seventh-day Adventist church. Let's compare the above clear statement of distinction between Father and Son with the current Seventh-day Adventist Statement of Belief about God.

---

[5] The fundamental principles of Seventh-day Adventists as expressed above appeared in the Adventist Year book every year until 1914. The year that Ellen White died, these Fundamental Principles ceased to appear until the revised statement drafted by F.M. Wilcox and possibly F.D. Nichol suddenly appeared in the 1931 year book. "However it originated, **"realizing that the General Conference Committee—or any other church body—would never accept the document in the form in which it was written, Elder Wilcox, with full knowledge of the group, handed the Statement directly to Edson Rogers, the General Conference statistician, who published it in the 1931 edition."** - Fritz Guy. *Uncovering the Origins of the Statement of 27 Fundamental Beliefs*. The 1931 statement reads: 2. That the Godhead, or Trinity, consists of the Eternal Father, a personal, spiritual Being, omnipotent, omnipresent, omniscient, infinite in wisdom, and love; the Lord Jesus Christ, the Son of the Eternal Father, through whom all things were created and through whom the salvation of the redeemed hosts will be accomplished; the Holy Spirit, the third person of the Godhead, the great regenerating power in the work of redemption. Matt. 28:19.

Trinity: **There is one God: Father, Son, and Holy Spirit, a unity of three co-eternal Persons**. God is immortal, all-powerful, all-knowing, above all, and ever present. **He** is infinite and beyond human comprehension, yet known through **His** self-revelation. **He** is forever worthy of worship, adoration, and service by the whole creation.

If this declaration about God is true then we would have to read 1 Corinthians 8:6 in the following way:

But to us there is but one triune God, the Trinity, of whom are all things, and we in him; by whom are all things, and we by him.

The Trinity is designed to destroy the "Of Whom" and "By Whom" distinctions of Father and Son which then flattens the divine pattern for living in the family, the church and the community.

Counterfeit Pattern: Broken Cords

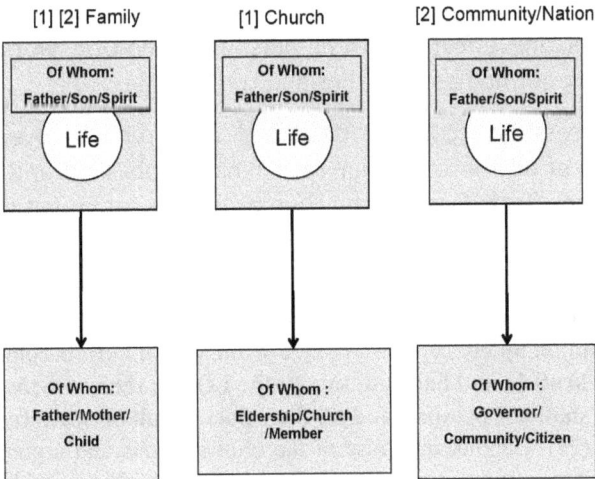

[1] [2] Family	[1] Church	[2] Community/Nation
Of Whom: Father/Son/Spirit Life	Of Whom: Father/Son/Spirit Life	Of Whom: Father/Son/Spirit Life
↓	↓	↓
Of Whom: Father/Mother/ Child	Of Whom : Eldership/Church /Member	Of Whom : Governor/ Community/Citizen

[1] = Priest [2] = Magistrate/Governor

The removal of the "Of Whom" and "By Whom" distinctions also removes the flow of the channel. Rather than clearly coming from the Father through the Son, it could originate in any one of them or all at the same time and everything becomes an incomprehensible mystery.

As an example you may read in the book of Judges how Israel turned away from the God with a distinct "Of Whom" and "By Whom" structure to Baal worship. (Judges 2:9,10). Notice how the family relations become confused, men became ruled by passion as in the case of Samson and others. Men also lost their sensitivity to the women in their lives as seen in the life of Jephthah in Judges 11. As children are born into families that no longer bless, then tyrants such as Abimelech (Judges 9) are developed. In other situations they become fearful, as in the case of Barak, who could not fight without a woman leading him (Judges 4).

Our church is going through the same process since we have embraced the Trinity with a counterfeit divine pattern of three identical beings, as opposed to Source and Channel as revealed in 1 Corinthians 8:6. We are seeing the number of men who can lead in our churches decreasing, marriage breakups increasing, the commissioning of female pastors on the rise, and the distinction between male and female increasingly blurred. All these things are symptoms of the desolating effects of three-persons-in-one-God worship; it is desolating our homes, churches and communities.

This process is accurately described by Jeremiah revealing the breaking of all the cords our Father has established and how the desolation affects families, the church, and the community:

> **Jer 10:20-25** My tabernacle is spoiled, and all **my cords are broken**: my children are gone forth of me, and they are not: there is none to stretch forth my tent any more, and to set up my curtains. (21) **For the pastors are become brutish, and have not sought the LORD: therefore they shall not prosper, and all their flocks shall be scattered.** (22) Behold, the noise of the bruit is come, and a great commotion out of the north country,[Babylon] to make the cities of Judah desolate, and a den of dragons. (23) O LORD, I know that **the way of man is not in himself:** it is not in man that walketh to direct his steps. (24) O LORD, correct me, but with judgment; not in thine anger, lest thou bring me to nothing. (25) Pour out thy fury upon the heathen that know thee not, and upon the families that call not on thy name: for they have eaten up Jacob, and

devoured him, and consumed him, and have made his habitation desolate.

The call of Elijah is a call to turn our hearts back to the true God of Israel, the God who is revealed at the heart of the Ten Commandments:

> **Mal 4:4-6** Remember ye the law of Moses my servant, which I commanded unto him in Horeb for all Israel, with the statutes and judgments. (5) Behold, I will send you Elijah the prophet before the coming of the great and dreadful day of the LORD: And he shall turn the heart of the fathers to the children, and the heart of the children to their fathers, lest I come and smite the earth with a curse.

The work of Elijah is a work of restoring the true God of Israel and a call to reflect our God in our families, our churches and our communities.

> **Luke 1:16-17** And many of the children of Israel shall he turn to the Lord their God. (17) And he shall go before him in the spirit and power of Elias, to turn the hearts of the fathers to the children, and the disobedient to the wisdom of the just; to make ready a people prepared for the Lord.

The turning of hearts involves recognition of parents by children and recognition by parents to bless. Turning people from disobedience involves people returning to a respect for their church and community leaders and for these leaders to recognise their need to bless and protect those under their care. The work of Elijah does not call men to free themselves from all human authority but rather to seek to restore that authority to the divine pattern. Let us join together in prayer for the power and spirit of Elijah to show us how to restore the divine pattern in our homes, churches and communities.

4. Blessing and Cursing

As we look more closely at the divine pattern through the Scriptures we see a picture emerge of how the "Of Whom" and "By Whom" parts of the pattern relate to each other. Our Father in Heaven is a God of blessing. Notice what the Bible says:

> **Num 23:19-20** God is not a man, that he should lie; neither the son of man, that he should repent: hath he said, and shall he not do it? or hath he spoken, and shall he not make it good? (20) Behold, I have received commandment to bless: and he hath blessed; and I cannot reverse it.

And again:

> **James 1:17** Every good gift and every perfect gift is from above, and cometh down from the Father of lights, with whom is no variableness, neither shadow of turning.

One of the key points for us to remember is that it is the joy, privilege and duty for the "Of Whom" to bless the "By Whom." We also note that the strength of the blessing is measured by the respect of the "By Whom" for the "Of Whom."

This blessing resides on a scale of degree that can switch into a curse. As love, honour, respect and obedience shift to dishonour, disrespect and disobedience, the channel moves from blessing to cursing. When a person moves against someone that God has ordained as an authority in his or her life, the blessing that should have been received turns into a curse. Note carefully these texts:

22

The Divine Pattern

Exod 20:5-6 …visiting the iniquity of the fathers upon the children unto the third and fourth generation of them that hate me; And shewing mercy unto thousands of them that love me, and keep my commandments.

Gen 12:3 And I will bless them that bless thee, and curse him that curseth thee: and in thee shall all families of the earth be blessed.

The channel where this principle is most powerful is where the origin of the "By Whom" comes directly from the "Of Whom."

1 Cor 11:3 But I would have you know, that the head of every man is Christ; and the head of the woman is the man; and the head of Christ is God.

Prov 17:6 Children's children are the crown of old men; and the glory of children are their fathers.

This channel is so powerful that it contains the power of life and death.

Matt 4:4 But he answered and said, It is written, Man shall not live by bread alone, but by every word that proceedeth out of the mouth of God.

John 6:63 It is the spirit that quickeneth; the flesh profiteth nothing: the words that I speak unto you, they are spirit, and they are life.

Prov 18:21 Death and life are in the power of the tongue: and they that love it shall eat the fruit thereof.

Every child lives by the life of his father. Ellen White, *Mount of Blessing*, page 78.

The Father's Words are life to us and His Word flows to us through the threefold cord that He has ordained to bless and protect us. The most urgent and critical blessing that our Father wants to send us is found in these words:

Matt 3:17 And lo a voice from heaven, saying, This is my beloved Son, in whom I am well pleased.

This blessing that Christ received from the Father is passed to us.

Eph 1:6 To the praise of the glory of his grace, wherein he hath made us accepted in the beloved.

Isn't it wonderful to know that the thrill that Jesus felt when He heard

His Father tell Him how much He loved Him can flow to us? Let us remember that these words of the Father are only as powerful as the authority we perceive that the Father has over His Son. Within the Trinity, the Father has delegated authority, meaning that the Spirit and Son voted the Father into His position. Yet the Bible reveals that the Father has absolute authority over His Son; therefore His words of blessing are absolute. That absolute blessing can be ours through Christ. How I pray that we can see the heart of the gospel in knowing God is the Father of Christ and that Christ is the Son of God.[1] It is the only way we can truly know that we are accepted in the Beloved and that His blessing is absolute.

We note carefully how Christ was enabled to receive the Father's blessing:

> **John 5:19** Then answered Jesus and said unto them, Verily, verily, I say unto you, The Son can do nothing of himself, but what he seeth the Father do: for what things soever he doeth, these also doeth the Son likewise.

> **John 5:30** I can of mine own self do nothing: as I hear, I judge: and my judgment is just; because I seek not mine own will, but the will of the Father which hath sent me.

> **John 8:29** And he that sent me is with me: the Father hath not left me alone; for I do always those things that please him.

> **Psa 40:8** I delight to do thy will, O my God: yea, thy law is within my heart.

> **John 15:10** If ye keep my commandments, ye shall abide in my love; even as I have kept my Father's commandments, and abide in his love.

In the life of Christ we see that the key to drawing down a blessing is to keep the words of the "Of Whom." As we keep the words of those appointed over us, this blesses the one who is appointed to protect and bless us.

> **Gen 12:3** …and I will bless them that bless thee

As the Son of God obeyed His Father, we see that Sarah obeyed her husband.

---

[1] "God is the Father of Christ; Christ is the Son of God." *Testimonies Vol. Eight*, page 268.

The Divine Pattern

> **1 Pet 3:6** Even as Sara obeyed Abraham, calling him lord: whose daughters ye are, as long as ye do well, and are not afraid with any amazement.

We see this again reflected in the parent and child pattern:

> **Eph 6:1** Children, obey your parents in the Lord: for this is right.

> **Col 3:20** Children, obey your parents in all things: for this is well pleasing unto the Lord.

And we see this principle expressed concerning all aspects of the threefold cord:

> **Rom 13:1,2** Let every soul be subject unto the higher powers. For there is no power but of God: the powers that be are ordained of God. Whosoever therefore resisteth the power, resisteth the ordinance of God: and they that resist shall receive to themselves damnation.

> **1 Pet 2:13-14** Submit yourselves to every ordinance of man for the Lord's sake: whether it be to the king, as supreme; (14) Or unto governors, as unto them that are sent by him for the punishment of evildoers, and for the praise of them that do well.

> **1 Thess 5:12-13** And we beseech you, brethren, to know them which labour among you, and are over you in the Lord, and admonish you; (13) And to esteem them very highly in love for their work's sake. And be at peace among yourselves.

As we behold the life of Jesus in the divine pattern, we see that life and blessing come from submission, respect, honour and keeping the words of the Authority that is over Him.

Again we repeat that the power of the blessing is directly measured by the power of respect and honour that the "By Whom" has for the "Of Whom." The more we treasure the words of the "Of Whom" the more they will bless us. The more we despise the "Of Whom" authority over us the more their words will judge and condemn us. The curse falls heavily upon us because rejecting the one that has authority over us causes us to emotionally condemn ourselves as well as feel at a distance from the authority figure. It also grates upon us to hear words of correction and disapproval rather than words of acceptance and approval. Words of approval bring blessing; words of disapproval bring a curse.

A good example of this process is found in the story of Cain. Cain disobeyed God by not bringing the correct sacrifice in worship. Then God directly points out Cain's error and encourages him to do the right thing. This attempt to correct Cain only intensified his anger to the point where he killed his brother for appealing to him to do the right thing. The curse falls upon Cain heavily. Why? Was it because God made him suffer? No, it was Cain's own sense of justice that caused him to feel that he lived without Heaven's approval. Notice carefully the marginal reading of Cain's response to God when he says:

> **Gen 4:13** And Cain said unto the LORD, My punishment is greater than I can bear.

If you read the margin, it says, "My iniquity is greater than can be forgiven." This means that Cain felt so bad that he no longer believed that God could accept him. This is the heart of the curse. When we disobey God and His delegated authorities, we are building a stronger and stronger sense that we are not approved or accepted by Heaven. There is no escape from this principle.

There are many who try to escape God's appointed authorities by asking the same question as the lawyer who wished to justify himself by asking, "Who is my neighbour?" So today, multitudes respond with, "Who is an authority in my life?" Many claim that the Bible alone is their authority, yet that very authority condemns their claim. God has placed a threefold cord of authority in our life to bless us; the Scriptures are clear on this. The Bible alone is the seed or "Of Whom" authority, but God has placed a threefold cord of "By Whom" or nurturing authorities in our lives for our protection and blessing. If we reject them then we are rejecting God's authority and shall receive a curse.

A natural question that arises in respect to this channel is: "What do I do when someone in my channel of authority asks me to do something contrary to the Word of God? What do I do when an authority figure rejects God and lives an immoral life? Am I still subject to their authority?" This is the question we will turn to next because all of us face this question at some point, and it is important to know how we should biblically respond.

Section 2. The Divine Pattern
When Leaders Fail

5. Responding to Apostasy

Many have heard of the familiar proverb that an ounce of prevention is worth a pound of cure, and this is certainly the case when living within the threefold cord of God's blessing. In our last chapter we spoke about how those who are under authority are blessed when they respect and obey authority. This then raises the question of what shall we do if a person in authority asks us to do things that are not revealed in God's Word or if they themselves engage in activities that are not of God.

Praying for Leaders

The first thing we should seek to do is prevent these situations from occurring through our prayers and our submissive spirit towards those in authority. When we have identified who the authority figures are in our lives, we should pray for them that God will bless them and give them wisdom, patience and discernment to properly execute their role. This is the counsel given us in the Bible:

> **1 Tim 2:1-2** I exhort therefore, that, first of all, supplications, prayers, intercessions, and giving of thanks, be made for all men; (2) For kings, and for all that are in authority; that we may lead a quiet and peaceable life in all godliness and honesty.

Do we regularly pray for our parents that God will bless them, their health and all they do? Do we pray that our parents will bless us with their words and acts of kindness? Through our prayers we can draw down blessings upon ourselves and our children and this is how our Father in Heaven would have it.

Do we faithfully pray for our church leaders, our pastor and the elders in the local church? Do we pray that our Father will give them peace, joy and the love of Christ? What about our local community leaders and government leaders? Do we pray for them? Do we hold them up before the Lord and pray for their families and their protection? These things are the duty of every Christian. Yet is this duty widely practiced? Not that I have seen. Why is this the case? It is another example of Satan's counterfeit divine pattern that flattens the authority structure. When we do not see that we are in a threefold cord of authority, we don't sense our need to pray for those over us, because we may not actually believe they are over us. If we do believe they are over us in some fashion, we often still do not see them as a channel of blessing for us.

When leaders grow weary from Satan's attacks, we need men like Aaron and Hur to hold up the arms of our leaders and support them and encourage them. Do we send cards of thanks to our leaders when there is opportunity to do it? Do we thank them for the good things they are doing? Leaders need encouragement and they need our prayers. All those who follow the divine pattern will remember those in authority over them and will seek to bless them through their acts of kindness and gracious spirit.

This process is important because if a leader falls, people should ask themselves, "have I faithfully prayed for this leader?" "Have I encouraged this leader?" If we can't answer honestly that we have then we should also repent for our own failure to do the tasks we ought to have done. It is Satan's studied aim to cause those under authority to cease their prayers for that authority. He can then tempt that leader to sin and then move the people against the leader with gossip, accusations and contempt.

If we have been faithfully praying for a leader and our hearts have developed affection for them through that process we will be shielded from the spirit of rebellion and discontent when we witness the fall of a leader. Those who are quick to mark the sins of a leader reveal that they have been slow to pray for and uphold that leader in their affections.

When Leaders Fail

Let us now come to the case where a leader has failed. Let us remind ourselves of some of the divine pattern situations where this could apply.

Source – Of Whom	Channel – By Whom	References
Father	Son	1 Cor 8:6; 1 Cor 11:3; Heb 1:1-3
Husband	Wife	Gen 3:16; 1 Cor 11:3; Eph 5:25; 1 Pet 3:1
Father	Mother	Ex 20:12; Eph 6:1; Col 3:20
Mother	Children	1 Tim 2:15
Christ	Husband	1 Cor 11:3
Christ	Church	Eph 5:25
Prophet	Priest	Ex 4:16; Lev 8:36
Elder/Pastors	Flock	1 Pet 5:2; 1 Thess 5:12,13
King/ Governor	Subjects/ Citizens	Rom 13:1-3; 1 Pet 2:13,14
Bible	Spirit of Prophecy	RH Jan 20, 1903 "Lesser Light"
Bible	Pastor/Elder	2 Tim 4:2; 1 Pet 5:2

As we noted previously, the "By Whom" person receives a blessing when they respect and obey the "Of Whom" person in authority over them. When we have a situation where an authority figure seeks to compel us by force to do something contrary to the Bible then we must respectfully state that we are not able to do this. Here are some Biblical examples:

> **Dan 3:14,16-18** Nebuchadnezzar spake and said unto them, Is it true, O Shadrach, Meshach, and Abednego, do not ye serve my gods, nor worship the golden image which I have set up? ... (16) Shadrach, Meshach, and Abednego, answered and said to the king, O Nebuchadnezzar, we are not careful to answer thee in this matter. (17) If it be so, our God whom we serve is able to deliver us from the burning fiery furnace, and he will deliver us out of thine hand, O king. (18) But if not, be it known unto thee, O king, that we will not serve thy gods, nor worship the golden image which thou hast set up.

Gen 39:7-8 And it came to pass after these things, that his master's wife cast her eyes upon Joseph; and she said, Lie with me. (8) But he refused, and said unto his master's wife, Behold, my master wotteth not what is with me in the house, and he hath committed all that he hath to my hand;

Acts 4:18-19 And they called them, and commanded them not to speak at all nor teach in the name of Jesus. (19) But Peter and John answered and said unto them, Whether it be right in the sight of God to hearken unto you more than unto God, judge ye.

In the above cases, God's people were asked to go contrary to Scripture which they would not do. Instead they were willing to face the consequences of obedience to the higher authority. This same test will face God's people in the near future when a Sunday Law is made universal.

Yet most situations with leadership do not involve a direct command to violate one's conscience, but rather a case of the leaders own failure to fulfil their role faithfully. In such cases here are some Biblical examples.

"Of Whom"	"By Whom"	Example
Potiphar	Joseph	Served faithfully
Eli	Hannah	Prayer in the Temple
Saul	David	Not touch the Lord's anointed
Elijah	Ahab	Ran before chariot
Daniel	Nebuchadnezzar	Food test/telling the dream

Joseph served his pagan master faithfully and did his best to bring blessing to his home. In the case of Hannah, Eli rebuked her for being drunk and she meekly replied, "No, my lord," and explained her situation. She did not turn and rebuke the priest for being lax with his sons and causing difficulties with the sacrifices. Even though David was anointed by Samuel to replace Saul, David would not raise his hand to remove Saul. He would not touch the Lord's anointed. Even though Elijah was a prophet and in some respects above Ahab, he still showed respect for the King of Israel by running before his chariot through the driving rain. In the case of Daniel, he showed discretion regarding unclean food by asking to be put to the test and in regard to the dream in Daniel 4 we see the real concern of Daniel for his king.

> **Dan 4:19** Then Daniel, whose name was Belteshazzar, was astonied for one hour, and his thoughts troubled him. The king spake, and said, Belteshazzar, let not the dream, or the interpretation thereof, trouble thee. Belteshazzar answered and said, My lord, the dream be to them that hate thee, and the interpretation thereof to thine enemies.

The king knew that Daniel cared for him and as a result trusted him. Even though this was the man who destroyed his home and took him captive, he still served him faithfully with a submissive spirit and was blessed as a result. The key in all these situations can be expressed through this counsel to one example of the divine pattern:

> **1 Pet 3:1-4** Likewise, ye wives, be in subjection to your own husbands; that, if any obey not the word, they also may without the word be won by the conversation of the wives; (2) While they behold your chaste conversation coupled with fear. (3) Whose adorning let it not be that outward adorning of plaiting the hair, and of wearing of gold, or of putting on of apparel; (4) But let it be the hidden man of the heart, in that which is not corruptible, even the ornament of a meek and quiet spirit, which is in the sight of God of great price.

In the case of a wife who has an unbelieving husband, she is to serve him faithfully seeking every way possible to bless and honour her husband. Through this process, the heart of the husband will hopefully soften and he will be impressed by the honour of his wife and he will give his heart to the Lord. Peter also gives counsel in other situations:

> **1 Pet 2:13-16** Submit yourselves to every ordinance of man for the Lord's sake: whether it be to the king, as supreme; (14) Or unto governors, as unto them that are sent by him for the punishment of evildoers, and for the praise of them that do well. (15) For so is the will of God, that with well doing ye may put to silence the ignorance of foolish men: (16) As free, and not using your liberty for a cloke of maliciousness, but as the servants of God.

The Bible counsels us that we are to have a submissive spirit that honours those in leadership and through this process we can put to silence the ignorance of foolish men.

This process of submission to a leader is a gentle means of reminding them that they are a leader and that it is their duty to bless. The person in submission will also be praying for that leader and asking for a blessing through them. Our God in Heaven who holds the king's heart in His hand can turn it and convict it to grant a blessing. The spirit of submission by its very nature draws down a blessing, whereas the spirit of rebuke sends the leader a message that "I am equal to you" or in fact "superior to you because my assessment of the situation is superior to yours." This is why the Bible says:

> **1 Tim 5:1** Rebuke not an elder, but entreat him as a father; and the younger men as brethren;

> **Exodus 22:28** Thou shalt not revile the gods (judges), nor curse the ruler of thy people.

It is a violation of the divine pattern for a person under authority to rebuke, revile or curse that authority. Only one equal to or above that authority figure can administer a direct rebuke. If we see a minister or elder teaching something that we believe is not Biblical, we must follow the divine pattern and approach them in a spirit of submission and gently appeal to them to consider what the Bible teaches. It is not our calling or duty to prove them wrong or expose them in front of a congregation. Satan is keen for members to elevate themselves to the level of the authority figure over them and to speak to them as if they were the authority. This destroys the channel of blessing and exposes people to Satan's attacks.

When a person directly challenges an authority over them, they are disrespecting that authority, and disrespect for authority brings a curse upon the person doing the rebuking. Remember what God told Abraham:

> **Gen 12:3** And I will bless them that bless thee, and curse him that curseth thee: and in thee shall all families of the earth be blessed.

We need to be very careful about how we speak about those in authority. Speaking badly of authority figures brings a curse upon us and our families. As Jude says:

> **Jude 1:8** Likewise also these filthy dreamers defile the flesh, despise dominion, and speak evil of dignities.

When we "despise dominion, and speak evil of dignities" we break the divine pattern and bring a tide of curse upon ourselves and those under our care. As those under our authority behold how we treat those in authority over us, they will be influenced by the same spirit and start to treat us in a similar manner. Once this spirit enters into a community, it will burst apart at some point fracturing along personality lines. This is the curse of those who "speak evil of dignities" and those in authority over them.

These principles are vitally important for us to consider in our current church situation. Many of us are under deep conviction that our leadership has turned away from the God of the Bible. How we respond to this sad situation needs to be carefully considered. Are we following the divine pattern in dealing with these things? At this point the question is often raised, "What is the church?" It is this subject that we want to turn to next.

6. Identifying the Church

Placing ourselves correctly in our communities means that we need to identify who the people and institutions are that we are to respect. We also need to identify those who are under our care and therefore protect and bless them. Living in western society has flattened many aspects of the divine pattern and blurred the channel system for many. Even so, most of us can identify two cords of the threefold cord.

Most of us can identify our parents or guardians from childhood, and the civil authorities in our lives such as government, police and magistrates are easy to identify. What is not so easy for many people to identify is the church authority in their lives. As part of the threefold cord, we need to clearly identify the church so we can know who to approach, appeal to and pray for.

We receive personal blessing through feeding on the Word of God individually and by following the divine pattern in our families and communities, but there is also a blessing that comes through God's church. The blessing that comes through God's church is the blessing that was given to Abraham.

> **Gen 12:2-3** And I will make of thee a great nation, and I will bless thee, and make thy name great; and thou shalt be a blessing: (3) And I will bless them that bless thee, and curse him that curseth thee: and in thee shall all families of the earth be blessed.

The children of Israel were the recipients of the promises of God including the covenants. The most vital part of this covenant included:

Heb 8:9-11 Not according to the covenant that I made with their fathers in the day when I took them by the hand to lead them out of the land of Egypt; because they continued not in my covenant, and I regarded them not, saith the Lord. (10) For this is the covenant that I will make with the house of Israel after those days, saith the Lord; I will put my laws into their mind, and write them in their hearts: and I will be to them a God, and they shall be to me a people: (11) And they shall not teach every man his neighbour, and every man his brother, saying, Know the Lord: for all shall know me, from the least to the greatest.

Please note that this covenant was made with the house of Israel. It is important to realise that when Israel as a nation ceased to be God's channel of blessing, the connection to God's original promise to Abraham was transferred to the Christian church.[1]

Gal 3:16,29 Now to Abraham and his seed were the promises made. He saith not, And to seeds, as of many; but as of one, And to thy seed, which is Christ.... (29) And if ye be Christ's, then are ye Abraham's seed, and heirs according to the promise.

We know that God's church under the leadership of the apostles spread quickly throughout the world, but soon came under intense persecution. This drove the church into the wilderness where she was protected by God for 1260 years.

Rev 12:6 And the woman fled into the wilderness, where she hath a place prepared of God, that they should feed her there a thousand two hundred and threescore days.

When the 1260 year period ended, the remnant of God's people came forth to proclaim the judgement hour message. This group is identified as keeping the commandments of God and the faith of

---

[1] "Christ must be the ground of our hope; for only through Him can we be heirs to eternal life. An immortal inheritance is presented to us on certain conditions. We cannot inherit a possession in this world unless we have a title that is without a flaw, and our right to an inheritance in the world to come, must also be clearly proved through a faultless title. **The line through which the heavenly inheritance is to come is plainly revealed in the Word of God. We must come under the provisions of the Abrahamic covenant**, and the requirements are, 'If ye be Christ's, then are ye Abraham's seed, and heirs according to the promise.'" *Messenger*, May 10, 1893. For more on this topic, see my sermon "You Shall be a Blessing." http://vimeo.com/15823129

Jesus.

> **Rev 12:17** And the dragon was wroth with the woman, and went to make war with the remnant of her seed, which keep the commandments of God, and have the testimony of Jesus Christ.

It is vitally important to remember that this channel of blessing comes through Abraham. It is therefore important that we examine closely the key principles of his worship system which will then help us identify who are the true spiritual descendants of Abraham. I outline in detail these principles in chapter 11 of my book *Life Matters,* but for the scope of this book, I will simply provide the summary as reflected first with Abraham and then with Israel.

Abraham	Israel
1. Family Structure (Gen 18:19)	1. The 5th commandment restored the family structure. The release from slavery gave families more time to spend together. Inheritance determined by family genealogy.
2. Nomadic Rural Dwellers (Heb 11:8-10)	2. Israel returned to a rural setting in the wilderness living in tents.
3. Identity by Parental Blessing (Gen 12:2)	3. God promised to bless Israel if faithful. The 5th commandment concerning parents restored the family blessing channel.
4. Observe Sabbath and Commandments (Gen 26:5)	4. God gave the commandments on Mt Sinai and taught them about the Sabbath through the collection of the manna.
5. Belief in Death and Resurrection (Heb 11:17-19)	5. The fourth commandment revealed God as the only source of life and the only One that keeps us alive. Without Him there is no life.
6. Saviour as Humble Life Restorer – Revealed in Slain Lamb (John 11:25)	6. A complete Sanctuary worship system was given to fully reveal the work of the coming Saviour and His work to teach us His commandments.
7. Focus of Worship on the Invisible (Heb 11:1,9-19)	7. The second commandment focused worship on the invisible.

The woman who comes out of the wilderness in Revelation 12 we understand to be the rise of the Seventh-day Adventist movement. Inspiration tells us in a number of places that the Adventist movement is repeating the history of Israel. Let us note carefully some of those parallels.

Israel	Church
1. Entered Egypt pure in faith but after a time slipped into apostasy. They went in with great knowledge and came out knowing very little – a bunch of slaves.	Apostolic Church started faithfully, but after a while slipped into apostasy – they went into the Dark Ages knowing the power of the gospel and came out struggling to release themselves from the enslaving teachings of Romanism.
2. Israel got mixed up with idolatry including bull and calf worship. Ex 32:1-4.	The church slipped into idolatry when Constantine mixed paganism with Christianity for the stability of the Roman Empire. The church soon after removed the second commandment which forbids idolatry.
3. In order for Israel to serve God properly again, they had to separate themselves from the Egyptians so they could keep His commandments. Ex 5:1-5; Ps 105:43-45.	God's true followers had to separate from the fallen church(es) so they could worship God in truth and keep His commandments. This occured under the preaching of the First and Second Angel's message from 1840-44.
4. God used Moses as His mouthpiece to instruct the children of Israel as to how they should best worship God. Moses died before they all went into Canaan – but Moses wrote down much instruction that carried them into the promised land.	God used Ellen White as His mouthpiece to instruct the church how they should best worship God. Ellen White died before the return of Christ, but wrote much instruction that will carry God's church into the Heavenly Canaan.

Israel	Church
5. Just as Israel came out of Egypt, they experienced the high of the Red Sea and then the bitter disappointment at Mara. Shortly after this they received instruction about the Ten Commandments.	Just as the Adventist church came out of Babylon/Egypt they experienced the high of the Midnight Cry and then the bitter disappointment of 1844. Shortly after they studied and found the full light on the Ten Commandments including the Sabbath.
6. The Sabbath was used by God as a test of loyalty to Him. Ex 16:4,23-28.	The Sabbath will be used as a test of loyalty to Him as shown in the First Angel's Message. Rev 14:6,7.
7. Israel was arranged into a complete organization ordered by 1000's then 100's then 50's then 10's. Ex 18:14-24.	The Adventist church was ordered by General Conference, by Unions, by Conference and by local church. Special instruction was given on this subject.
8. Special instruction was given on healthful living. Leviticus 11.	In 1863 Ellen White received a number of visions of this subject.
9. Worship was based around the Sanctuary. Exodus 25-40.	Worship is based around the Heavenly Sanctuary. Rev 11:19; 15:5.
10. Israel came to the edge of Canaan and received the message that God would give Canaan to them, but they rejected the message and wandered in the wilderness for 40 years. God took a new generation in to Canaan.	The Adventist Church received a special message in 1888 which could have enabled them to enter Heaven shortly after, but the message was largely rejected and we have been wandering ever since. God will bring a new generation into the Heavenly Canaan.

The Adventist Church was placed to receive the blessings of Abraham, because it emerged from the 1260 year period and then embraced the core components of that blessing system through worship of the true God, His commandments and His Sanctuary worship system.

Note carefully what inspiration says of the relationship Adventism has with the God of Heaven:

> **Commandment-keeping Adventists are occupying a peculiar, exalted position.** John viewed them in holy vision, and described them. "Here are they that keep the

commandments of God, and the faith of Jesus." **The Lord made a special covenant with his ancient Israel** if they would prove faithful: "Now, therefore, if ye will obey my voice indeed, and keep my covenant, then ye shall be a peculiar treasure unto me above all people; for all the earth is mine. And ye shall be unto me a kingdom of priests, and an holy nation." **And he thus addresses his commandment-keeping people in these last days**: "But ye are a chosen generation, a royal priesthood, an holy nation, a peculiar people; that ye should show forth the praises of him who hath called you out of darkness into his marvelous light." *Review and Herald*, September 7, 1886.

God has called His church in this day, as He called ancient Israel, to stand as a light in the earth. By the mighty cleaver of truth, the messages of the first, second, and third angels, He has separated them from the churches and from the world to bring them into a sacred nearness to Himself. He has made them the depositaries of His law and has committed to them the great truths of prophecy for this time. Like the holy oracles committed to ancient Israel, these are a sacred trust to be communicated to the world. *Testimonies, Volume 5*, page 455.

"The Lord spake unto Moses, saying, Speak thou also unto the children of Israel, saying, Verily My Sabbaths ye shall keep: for it is a sign between Me and you throughout your generations; that ye may know that I am the Lord that doth sanctify you. Ye shall keep the Sabbath therefore; for it is holy unto you: everyone that defileth it shall surely be put to death: for whosoever doeth any work therein, that soul shall be cut off from among his people. Six days may work be done; but in the seventh is the Sabbath of rest, holy to the Lord: whosoever doeth any work in the Sabbath day, he shall surely be put to death. Wherefore the children of Israel shall keep the Sabbath, to observe the Sabbath throughout their generations, for a perpetual covenant. It is a sign between Me and the children of Israel forever: for in six days the Lord made heaven and earth, and on the seventh day He rested, and was refreshed." Exodus 31:12-17. **Do not these words point us out as God's denominated people? and do they not declare to us that so long as time shall last, we are to cherish the sacred, denominational distinction placed upon us?** The children of Israel were to observe the Sabbath throughout their generations "for a perpetual covenant." The Sabbath has lost none of its meaning. It is still the sign between God and His people, and it will be so forever. *Testimonies, Volume 9*, page 17.

These inspired statements make it abundantly clear that God has placed the blessing of Abraham upon the Seventh-day Adventist movement. Yet these blessings poured upon the Seventh-day Adventist church have made her the special object of Satan's wrath. As the verse in Revelation 12:17 indicates:

> **Rev 12:17 And the dragon was wroth with the woman, and went to make war with the remnant of her seed,** which keep the commandments of God, and have the testimony of Jesus Christ.

This special attack has led Adventism to repeat the history of Israel.

> Satan's snares are laid for us as verily as they were laid for the children of Israel just prior to their entrance into the land of Canaan. **We are repeating the history of that people**. *Testimonies, Volume 5*, page 160.

If we study carefully Israel's history right upon the borders of Canaan, we see that the people fell into apostasy and participated in the false worship of the nations around them. If you study carefully *Patriarchs and Prophets*, chapter 41, "Apostasy at the Jordan", you can read what happened to Israel and hopefully discern the parallels for us today. The very fact that an apostasy has occurred within the Adventist movement actually confirms her special relationship to God rather than disproves it. Even as the disappointment of our pioneers confirmed their status through the parallel to the disappointment of the disciples at the death of Christ, so the current apostasy on the borders of the Heavenly Canaan confirms the parallel to ancient Israel who originally held a covenant status with God.

The prophet states concerning Israel[2]:

> They ventured upon the forbidden ground, and were entangled in the snare of Satan. Beguiled with music and dancing, and allured by the beauty of heathen vestals [daughters of Babylon], they cast off their fealty to Jehovah. As they united in mirth and feasting [acceptance by Protestant

---

[2] Comments in square brackets supplied

churches], indulgence in wine [false doctrine of the Trinity, nature of Christ, atonement etc] beclouded their senses and broke down the barriers of self-control. Passion had full sway; and having defiled their consciences by lewdness, they were persuaded to bow down to idols [the Trinity]. They offered sacrifice upon heathen altars and participated in the most degrading rites [Emergent church]. It was not long before the poison had spread, like a deadly infection, through the camp of Israel. Those who would have conquered their enemies in battle were overcome by the wiles of heathen women. The people seemed to be infatuated. **The rulers and the leading men were among the first to transgress,** and so many of the people were guilty that the apostasy became national. "Israel joined himself unto Baalpeor." *Patriarchs and Prophets*, page 454.

Zimri, one of the nobles of Israel, came boldly into the camp, accompanied by a Midianitish harlot, a princess "of a chief house in Midian," whom he escorted to his tent. Never was vice bolder or more stubborn. Inflamed with wine [false teaching], Zimri declared his "sin as Sodom," and gloried in his shame. *Patriarchs and Prophets*, page 455.

How was Israel awakened to her sin?

By swift-coming judgments the people were awakened to the enormity of their sin. A terrible pestilence broke out in the camp, to which tens of thousands speedily fell a prey. **God commanded that the leaders in this apostasy be put to death by the magistrates**. This order was promptly obeyed. The offenders were slain, then their bodies were hung up in sight of all Israel that the congregation, seeing the leaders so severely dealt with, might have a deep sense of God's abhorrence of their sin and the terror of His wrath against them. *Patriarchs and Prophets*, page 455.

Is there any reason to believe that the history will not be faithfully followed today? Have we not been told that we are repeating the history of Israel? God is not mocked and willful apostasy will meet with divine justice. That justice would not be carried out by members of the church as in the time of Israel, yet God will still ensure that such apostasy will be faithfully dealt with.

Those who rise in anger against our church leaders both fail to understand their position in the blessing structure and also fail to trust that God is not mocked. It is a fearful thing to fall into the hands of the living God.

My appeal to my church family is that we weep and plead for our leaders, for at present they are marked for certain destruction. The work of repentance and pleading before the Lord is not one that is desired by the carnal heart. There is no love in the carnal heart for our poor leaders, many of whom are facing certain death at present.

Let us place ourselves in a position as a wife does to her unbelieving husband and seek to win our leaders by our conduct. Those who rise in anger and connect this precious message of God's dear Son with aggression, calling the church Babylon, are doing the work of Satan to harden our leaders in their apostasy. "A soft answer turns away wrath" and "a word fitly spoken is like apples of gold in pictures of silver." Proverbs 15:1; 25:11.

7. Resting in the Channel

I distinctly remember praying an angry prayer to the Lord concerning what some of the church leaders were doing at the time. Some were allowing worldly music, staying silent on several standards issues and allowing dubious speakers to address our people. I was pouring out my heart to the Lord about these things with a deep sense of frustration towards the leadership for allowing these things to happen.

I can't recall exactly the impression that came to me, but the substance of it was that I was giving the leadership more power than I biblically should and this was driving much of my frustration. I was reminded that all authority comes from God and that He is not blinded to the failures of leadership. I saw that much of my anger was a lack of faith that God was in control of the situation.

On another occasion, I was feeling very hostile towards my father because of what I perceived to be an injustice on his part. I wanted his blessing on some subject but I ended up with a curse. Again as I poured out my frustration to the Lord, I was strongly impressed, "Your father is not God, and you expect of him more than he can give you. This is the source of your disappointment."

This has been a hard lesson for me to learn, but one that is vital if we are to be able to face the failures of leaders without our disappointment boiling over into rebellion.

Within the divine pattern, the Scriptures reveal several accounts where the "By Whom" person has tried to manipulate the "Of Whom" person to get what they desire. The case of Rebekah instructing Jacob to deceive his father to secure the birthright is a notable example. Isaac resisted the prophetic Word concerning the older serving the younger and moved to place the birthright upon Esau. Rebekah revealed her lack of faith in God, forgetting that He was the one who told her that Esau would serve Jacob. She moved to secure the blessing through deception and brought a terrible curse upon herself; she never saw Jacob again after he fled to his uncle's home.

Again we see how Rachel became hostile towards Jacob when she was unable to have children.

> **Gen 30:1** And when Rachel saw that she bare Jacob no children, Rachel envied her sister; and said unto Jacob, Give me children, or else I die.

Rachel fell into the trap of attributing to Jacob more power than he had causing her to act aggressively towards him. Rachel's aggression brought a swift curse from her husband, reminding her in a forceful manner that he was not God.

> **Gen 30:2** And Jacob's anger was kindled against Rachel: and he said, Am I in God's stead, who hath withheld from thee the fruit of the womb?

There are several examples in Scripture of people in subordinate positions who lacked trust that God was in control and tried to take things into their own hands thus bringing a curse upon themselves.

One example that I would like to share with you is the case of Ahithophel.

Ahithophel was one of David's counsellors and he was also the grandfather of Bathsheba. Compare 2 Sam 11:3 with 2 Sam 23:34. Ahithophel had good reason to feel frustrated with David for sleeping with his granddaughter and bringing sin upon Israel. He also could have sympathised with Absalom over David's lack of discipline when Amnon, Absalom's half-brother raped his sister. See 2 Sam 13.

It appeared to Ahithophel that David was going to get away with his sinful practices and so Ahithophel backed the rebellion of Absalom to take David's throne. The Scripture reveals that the Lord overturned the counsel of Ahithophel and David's men won the battle. Ahithophel knew his fate and before he could be found, he hanged himself. See 2 Sam17:1-23.

Ahithophel's plan was carefully crafted and he nearly succeeded in his plans, but since David was the Lord's anointed his plans ended in disaster. The case of Ahithophel has always stuck in my mind as a warning to those who would topple corrupt leadership without a thus saith the Lord.

In contrast to Ahithophel, David waited upon the Lord to deal with Saul. David had many more reasons to take the leadership from Saul than Absalom did from David. Yet David would not lay his hand upon the Lord's anointed. Even when he was anointed by Samuel to be king, he still waited for God to bring judgement on Saul. We see the depth of David's respect for authority when he mourned for Saul after his death and penned these words:

> **2 Sam 1:23** Saul and Jonathan were lovely and pleasant in their lives, and in their death they were not divided: they were swifter than eagles, they were stronger than lions.

A man who puts his trust in God can afford to be gracious to those who hate him. Saul hated David and tried for a long time to kill him and this is David's response. I pray his example will ring in our minds as we consider the current apostasy.

The key to resting in the blessing channel is to have an experiential knowledge of God and His Son. Those who study the Scriptures with discernment know that our Father is the source of all life and that nothing escapes His notice. They know that no man can have any power unless it was given him by God. This was Christ's secret when facing Pilate.

> **John 19:10,11** Then saith Pilate unto him, Speakest thou not unto me? knowest thou not that I have power to crucify thee, and have power to release thee? Jesus answered, Thou couldest have no power at all against me, except it were given thee from above: therefore he that delivered me unto thee hath the greater sin.

Jesus stood before Pilate and the might of Rome. He had been beaten, whipped and was staring death in the face. What Pilate was doing was weak, cowardly and corrupt. Jesus had the power to expose this corruption and set Himself free at any moment. At the very least He could have spoken to Pilate in a way to cause him to let Jesus go. Add to this that Jesus was brought before Pilate because of a corrupt

Church that was up to its neck in apostasy. Yet Jesus remained calm and measured with the knowledge:

> **John 19:11** "Thou couldest have no power at all against me, except it were given thee from above."

What a lesson is this for us! All power comes from God and not a sparrow falls to the ground without our Father's knowledge. We can rest in the channel of blessing knowing that:

> **Prov 21:1** The king's heart is in the hand of the LORD, as the rivers of water: he turneth it whithersoever he will.

Let us behold Christ, the submissive Son of God, who trusted His Father in all situations and was never moved to defend Himself even to save His own life. Here is the second secret of those who rest in the channel; they see that the Son of God does nothing of Himself. He does only what His Father commands and no more.

Let us also consider that at the heart of the great controversy is the issue of submitting to an authority that God has placed in our life. Lucifer refused to submit to the authority of Christ who was delegated by His Father as the Sovereign of Heaven. The spirit of resistance towards authority and the desire to expose, shame and humiliate those in authority is the very spirit of Satan himself. Such persons do not know Christ or the power of God.

The last thing I would mention that has helped me to rest in the channel of blessing is to discern the serpent's lie of inherent power that all are in danger of applying to leadership. One of the things that cause us to give too much power to leaders is our belief that leaders have power to do whatever they wish. The flip side of this is that we imagine that leaders have the power to give us the things we want. It was this type of thinking that led Israel to desire a king to be over them.

> **1 Sam 8:19-20** Nevertheless the people refused to obey the voice of Samuel; and they said, Nay; but we will have a king over us; (20) That we also may be like all the nations; and that our king may judge us, and go out before us, and fight our battles.

This concept of leadership is not part of the channel of blessing but rather is the spirit of Anti-Christ. It is the replacing of God with a human idol. Notice what the Lord said:

1 Sam 8:7 And the LORD said unto Samuel, Hearken unto the voice of the people in all that they say unto thee: for they have not rejected thee, but they have rejected me, that I should not reign over them.

In this case, the desire for a leader was turning a potential "By Whom" channel into the supreme "Of Whom" authority. This is exactly the same as what the Church of Rome has done through the Pope. The leader wields absolute authority in his own right. The investing of a man with such authority is the natural process of idolatry; the creation of a leader follows after the desire of the carnal heart, and the desire of the carnal heart is to rule independent of any other authority. The most subtle form of this idolatry is the Trinitarian belief that places Jesus as an independent yet co-equal ruler with the Father because of His own inherent qualities. The worship of the Adventist Trinitarian Jesus is the worship of a being who is not under absolute authority. The complete rejection of the inheritance of the Son is as much a rejection of the Father as Israel rejected Jehovah in the days of Samuel. Such worship can easily lead to the spirit of despotism as was manifested in Saul.

Resting in the channel is not only an acceptance of all the "By Whom" agencies God has placed in our life, but is also a rejection of any attempts to elevate any person to the position of supreme "Of Whom" status.

8. The Mantle for Confrontation

The more we bring ourselves into line with the divine pattern and the more we learn to honour the authorities God has placed in our lives, the more our motivation to see that leaders speak and do the right things will come from a recognition that this person is ordained to pass a portion of God's blessings to us.

If we sense that a leader is sliding into wrong teachings or practices, our hearts will be urgent to protect their reputation as a leader and will be praying that God will give them wisdom and blessing so they will not damage their leadership position with wrongdoing.

The spirit of anger that arises in people towards leaders for wrongdoing is rarely motivated by love for that leader. It may simply be the cry of pain from those cursed by the leader's wrong actions, or it may be the more complex situation of a person seeking to raise their position to a level equal to or above that leader. A spirit that is quick to report the failings of leadership is a spirit that despises the divine pattern. In most cases when we report on the failures of a leader, we are diminishing the level of respect in the minds of the people with whom we share the failures. We are reducing the power of the words of that leader and therefore we are reducing their ability to bless.

When a wife complains to others about the failings of her husband, she is reducing his authority to bless her. If she complains about him to her children, then she is diminishing his ability to bless them with his words. She is encouraging her children to scorn their father and ultimately her careless manner towards her husband's real or imaginary failures undermines her own authority with her children. In the same manner, a man who speaks negatively about the minister, government or police to his children is doing the same thing; he is dismantling parts of the threefold cord of protection.[1] When we disregard authority we are in great danger of destroying our children.[2] Note carefully:

> "Children, obey your parents in all things: for this is well pleasing unto the Lord." Children who dishonor and disobey their parents, and disregard their advice and instructions, can have no part in the earth made new. *Adventist Home*, page 295.

Let us consider carefully the Biblical directive for those who curse their parents:

> **Exod 21:17** And he that curseth his father, or his mother, shall surely be put to death.

In the times of Israel, cursing your parents was a crime punishable by death. What is the Lord trying to teach us by these things? Again notice how David responded to the man who claimed to have killed Saul, the Lord's anointed.

> **2 Sam 1:14-15** And David said unto him, How wast thou not afraid to stretch forth thine hand to destroy the LORD'S anointed? (15) And David called one of the young men, and said, Go near, and fall upon him. And he smote him that he died.

Do we begin to understand the seriousness of this situation? Do we begin to appreciate the life and death issues that are bound up in a

---

[1] "...it was not the design of God that the husband should have control, as head of the house, when he himself does not submit to Christ. He must be under the rule of Christ that he may represent the relation of Christ to the church." *Adventist Home*, page 117.

[2] Respect for authority includes those over us as well as those under us as indicated in this statement. "The father and mother are to be respected in the Christian home. The father is the priest and house-band of the home. The mother is the teacher of the little ones from their babyhood, and queen of the household. **Never is she to be slighted. Never are careless, indifferent words to be spoken to her before the children.** She is their teacher. In thought and word and deed the father is to reveal the religion of Christ, that his children may see plainly that he has a knowledge of what it means to be a Christian." *Review and Herald,* June 22, 1905

correct approach to those in authority? It is with these things in mind that Paul instructs us:

> **1 Tim 5:1** Rebuke not an elder, but entreat him as a father; and the younger men as brethren;

When we perceive that a leader may not be acting according to God's Word, we must act very carefully. If we receive a report from a single source concerning a leader, we cannot accept it.

> **Deut 19:15** One witness shall not rise up against a man for any iniquity, or for any sin, in any sin that he sinneth: at the mouth of two witnesses, or at the mouth of three witnesses, shall the matter be established.

If we pass on a report concerning a leader that has not been validated, then we are guilty of laying our hands on the Lord's anointed; we bring a terrible curse upon ourselves.

If we hear a pastor, leader or parent speak a word or do something that is not correct, our desire to safeguard their position will cause us to pray and make certain that we have observed something faulty in their conduct. Then because we love this leader we will go to them privately and enquire of them concerning the situation and whether we have understood the situation correctly. We should not speak to others about the matter in case we have misunderstood. If we speak to others then we are damaging the mantle of the Lord's anointed and we will bring a curse upon ourselves.

If the leader denies the report or indicates that we have misunderstood, we must leave the situation to the Lord. If the situation occurs again, then we might approach them again and appeal to them. If it is something concerning the teaching of the Bible, we should gently ask them to instruct us rather than demand them to prove their position. We should go to them believing that we may have missed something or have misunderstood or that we might be wrong. If we assume we are right then we are not open to their counsel and we will bring a curse upon ourselves.

If an issue persists and the leader is not responding after much prayer and pleading, then we should approach the elders and submit the request before them. Once we have submitted the evidence to the elders or the board, the responsibility is then moved to the elders or board. We have done all that we can to safeguard the reputation of the leader. During this process we may discover that we were wrong or received wrong information or that we had misunderstood what the Bible teaches. Through this process we can ensure that we have not placed a single needless doubt in anyone's mind concerning that leader.

It is with these thoughts in mind that we start to appreciate the proper procedure for approaching a leader in our community. We need to understand that only those under our authority can be confronted and commanded to alter their course. If a minister is acting incorrectly, then it is within the authority of his President to confront, and if need be, correct that minister for incorrect conduct. If a Conference President is guilty of misconduct, then a Union President or Division leader has the authority to confront and correct such a leader. Obviously, if a church leader engages in any civil crime then the police and government have the authority to charge and punish such a minister or church leader. This is how the threefold cord should operate.

If all these checks and balances fail and the entire structure becomes involved in apostasy and incorrect behaviour then the mantle of confrontation must be given directly to the person of God's choosing. Let us consider several Bible examples.

Event	Mantle of Authority	Confrontation
Slavery of children of Israel in Egypt.	Moses given mantle of authority to confront Pharaoh by the visit of the Lord in the burning bush and miracles with the leprosy and the serpent. Exodus 4.	Pharaoh confronted by Moses and Aaron and received judgements of plagues for refusing to listen. Exodus 5-11.
Apostasy in the time of the Judges. They forsook the Lord and served Baalim. Judges 2:9,10.	Angel of the Lord appeared to Gideon and commanded him to tear down his father's idol. Confirmed through consuming the food by fire. After this he received confirmation through the wet and dry fleece. Judges 6.	Gideon tore down his father's idol and later assembled the 300 to break the power of the Midianites.

Event	Mantle of Authority	Confrontation
Eli did not restrain his sons from polluting the sacrifices and engaging in immoral practices. 1 Sam 2:25-27.	A man of God appeared and predicted the destruction of Eli's house. The mantle of authority came through the specific details in the prophecy. (If a man predicted things and they did not come to pass he was to be put to death. So you wanted to be sure you were called. Deut 13:1-5.)	God confronted Eli through the unnamed man of God as well as a message to Samuel. The nature of events proved clearly the Lord was in it. Eli and his house perished exactly as was predicted. 1 Sam 4.
Saul's Apostasy.	Samuel was still operating as an established prophet. The Lord commanded him to anoint David as replacement. 1 Sam 15,16.	Samuel confronts Saul and predicted his demise. Samuel anoints David as replacement. 1 Sam 15,16.
David's sin with Bathsheba. 2 Sam 11.	Nathan was recognised as a prophet in Israel. 2 Sam 7:2. Also his detailed knowledge of David's sin and what would be the judgement revealed his prophetic voice.	Nathan confronts David with his crime and pronounces judgement on his house. 2 Sam 12.
Ahab's apostasy with Jezebel.	Elijah gives evidence of prophetic authority through the message that rain would not fall without the word of Elijah. 1 Kings 17:1.	Elijah confronts Israel at Mt. Carmel and shows who is the true God of Israel. 1 Kings 18.
Israel's apostasy just before Christ came. Abuse of sacrificial system. Bribery, corruption and use of civil power for religious purposes.	John confirmed as a prophet through the experience of Gabriel meeting Zacharias in Luke 1; as well as the prophecy of Isaiah 40, the voice of one crying in the wilderness.	John confronts the leaders of Israel and calls for repentance. Luke 3. He also confronted the civil authority of Herod. Matt 14.
Israel's apostasy at time of Christ.	Christ confirmed as prophet through 100's of prophecies as well as by his forerunner – John the Baptist.	Christ confronts the priesthood on many occasions and pronounces judgement upon them. Matt 23 for example.

Event	Mantle of Authority	Confrontation
Priest's suppression of Apostles preaching the name of Christ.	Christ placed the mantle of authority upon the Disciples. Mark 3:14. He also commanded them to preach the gospel and make disciples. Matt 28:19,20. They also received the former rain power and also did miracles. Acts 2.	The Apostles confronted the priesthood with the charge of putting Jesus to death and refused to stop speaking in the name of Jesus.

There are several points we could draw out from the example above. I want to highlight one aspect of the story of Gideon. Notice what Ellen White says:

> Gideon's father, Joash, who shared in the apostasy of his countrymen, had erected at Ophrah, where he dwelt, a large altar to Baal, at which the people of the town worshiped. Gideon was commanded to destroy this altar and to erect an altar to Jehovah over the rock on which the offering had been consumed, and there to present a sacrifice to the Lord. **The offering of sacrifice to God had been committed to the priests, and had been restricted to the altar at Shiloh; but He who had established the ritual service, and to whom all its offerings pointed, had power to change its requirements.** The deliverance of Israel was to be preceded by a solemn protest against the worship of Baal. Gideon must declare war upon idolatry before going out to battle with the enemies of his people. *Patriarchs and Prophets*, page 547.

The visitation by the angel of the Lord to Gideon allowed Gideon to offer a sacrifice to the Lord outside of Shiloh. Secondly, we note that before Israel could go to war with its enemies, there needed to be a protest concerning idolatry within the community of Israel. Before we can engage the enemies of Israel we need to have a protest concerning the idolatry occurring in Adventism. Gideon's protest was authorised by the Angel of the Lord. The next thing we notice is:

> Gideon dared not place himself at the head of the army without still further evidence that God had called him to his work, and that He would be with him. *Patriarchs and Prophets*, page 548.

Gideon faithfully made his protest and tore down his father's idol as the angel commanded. Again we state that Gideon was authorised to confront this idolatry because of the Angel of the Lord's direct command. Yet he did not automatically assume leadership of Israel after this. He asked the Lord to provide evidence of His leading.

The point we wish to make by these examples is that each time all other avenues had been exhausted, God authorised a person or persons to confront the existing blessing structure which had failed. It is a dangerous thing to quote portions of Scripture where men were called to confront a system in apostasy and ignore the fact that God clearly gave them this authority through:

1. Clear evidence the word spoken is prophetic.
2. A sequence of miracles or providential events.
3. Visitations from angels with instruction.
4. Authorisation from another prophet living or recorded in Scripture.

Our God does all things decently and in order. Before a person can speak with commanding authority, there must be evidence that the person speaking has the authority to confront someone that normally would not be possible. These things must also be confirmed by more than one witness.

This is a lesson of utmost importance for us today who are facing wide scale apostasy. To rise up without authority is to break the divine pattern and to bring a curse upon those who do it.

For those whom God has granted to find the truth of God's Son, we have been granted to:

1. Engage in a work of repentance for the sins of anti-typical Israel.

2. We have been granted the right from Scripture to confess a belief in the only begotten Son within the precincts of our authority.

3. We have the need to safeguard the reputations of our leaders and pray for them that God will help them.

4. We are to wait for clear evidences of authority from Heaven before appeal can turn to confrontation.

The Divine Pattern

The first step of any reformation involves repentance. It is not enough to simply accept the truth of the Father and Son and then start telling others. We must confess the sin of the Trinity and plead before the Lord for forgiveness.

> There is need today of such a revival of true heart religion as was experienced by ancient Israel. Repentance is the first step that must be taken by all who would return to God. No one can do this work for another. We must individually humble our souls before God and put away our idols. When we have done all that we can do, the Lord will manifest to us His salvation. *Patriarchs and Prophets*, page 590.

As we engage the work of repentance, the Lord will show us the next step to take. He who runs before the time appointed does not represent the God of Israel or His divine pattern. Any man or woman who dares to raise their voice against the Lord's anointed and diminish their authority in the eyes of the people without a clear evidence of their calling, should be pled with to cease and repent. If they refuse, they are to be rejected and avoided.

So how will we know that God has given such authority? In the time we are now living, no one can claim to have been authorised by an existing or previous prophet. If a person received a visitation from an angel, other evidence would need to accompany such claims, as any person could claim to have had an angel visit. A person could become established through a series of predictions that take place. Also it is possible for a series of miracles or providential events to occur, but such things must be combined with a message that agrees with the platform of truth given to our pioneers. The spirit that provides miracles and providential events must always be tested and the best way to test these spirits is by the message they bring.

> **1 John 4:1** Beloved, believe not every spirit, but try the spirits whether they are of God: because many false prophets are gone out into the world.

> **Isa 8:20** To the law and to the testimony: if they speak not according to this word, it is because there is no light in them.

> **Deut 13:1-3** If there arise among you a prophet, or a dreamer of dreams, and giveth thee a sign or a wonder, (2) And the sign or the wonder come to pass, whereof he spake

unto thee, saying, Let us go after other gods, which thou
hast not known, and let us serve them; (3) Thou shalt not
hearken unto the words of that prophet, or that dreamer
of dreams: for the LORD your God proveth you, to know
whether ye love the LORD your God with all your heart
and with all your soul.

From my personal study, I believe that authority to confront our
current apostasy will grow out of a swelling cry of the love and joy
found in the begotten Son combined with a spirit of repentance
for our church, our leaders and ourselves for being involved in this
apostasy. As we move closer toward the divine pattern and uphold
our leaders in prayer, then I believe a series of providential events
will be given from Heaven to indicate that God has taken things into
His hands.

I believe there is good instruction for us that relates to the coming of
the fourth angel of Revelation. This instruction does not speak to the
issues directly relating to the Adventist church but to giving the Three
Angels Messages to the world. Yet there is a principle for us here:

In every generation God has sent His servants to rebuke sin,
both in the world and in the church. But the people desire
smooth things spoken to them, and the pure, unvarnished
truth is not acceptable. Many reformers, in entering upon
their work, determined to exercise great prudence in
attacking the sins of the church and the nation. They hoped,
by the example of a pure Christian life, to lead the people
back to the doctrines of the Bible. **But the Spirit of God
came upon them as it came upon Elijah,** moving him
to rebuke the sins of a wicked king and an apostate people;
they could not refrain from preaching the plain utterances
of the Bible-- doctrines which they had been reluctant to
present. They were impelled to zealously declare the truth
and the danger which threatened souls. **The words which
the Lord gave them** they uttered, fearless of consequences,
and the people were compelled to hear the warning. Thus
the message of the third angel will be proclaimed. As the
time comes for it to be given with greatest power, the Lord
will work through humble instruments, leading the minds of
those who consecrate themselves to His service. The laborers
will be qualified rather by the unction of His Spirit than by
the training of literary institutions. Men of faith and prayer

will be constrained to go forth with holy zeal, declaring the words which God gives them. *Great Controversy*, page 606.

In this case, men will indeed receive authority from Heaven as they come under conviction of the truths of the Word of God. Their message will bear the credentials of Heaven. The Spirit will manifest in their lives in such a way that the followers of truth will mark the providence that attends them. This is not a work that man can produce himself, it only occurs as the Spirit of God comes upon them as we have witnessed by previous Bible examples.

Now is the time for repentance, prayer, fasting and weeping. Now is the time to wait upon the Lord and plead for Israel. Soon the anti-type of the apostasy at the Jordan will fall upon us. May we not be faced with the question from the Son of David:

> **2 Sam 1:14** How wast thou not afraid to stretch forth thine hand to destroy the LORD'S anointed?

9. Making an Appeal

For those of us who hold membership within the Seventh-day Adventist Church, we have a responsibility to our leaders and their families to make an appeal to them regarding what we have found in Scripture concerning the Son of God.

From what we have examined in previous chapters, there are a number of reasons why we must do this:

1. Our love for those in authority over us.
2. Our concern for their reputation.
3. Our need for their blessing and protection in our lives.
4. A need to make certain that we have not fallen into error.

I say these are the reasons that we must make an appeal, because there are many who are vulnerable to the practice of staying silent and seeking to quietly approach other church members to win them first. When a person comes under the conviction that they have found truth in the knowledge of the Son of God, that person is immediately tested as to whether they really believe this truth by submitting to the divine pattern and approaching their leaders in a spirit of submission and grace.

A failure to speak to your church leaders about these things after you have become fully convinced in your mind that it is the truth reveals that you do not love those in authority over you. Making an appeal to our leaders reveals that we have embraced this message in the correct way and for the right motives.

There can be many wrong reasons to embrace an idea contrary to the belief of those in authority over us. A spirit of independence and self-will can be attracted to contrary views. Men can even be attracted to the truth for the wrong reason of using it as a pretext to rebel against the channel of authority.

It is my observation that there are people who have been attracted to the truth of the Son of God in order that they might exalt themselves and engage in a campaign against God's remnant church. Satan delights exceedingly when people embrace that which is right based on a motive of that which is wrong. He knows that the spirit of independence combined with the truth of the Son of God is well placed to offend many who would otherwise study this teaching.

Let us come back to this question of making an appeal. In my reading of Scripture, once we come to a knowledge of this truth and as we allow this truth to manifest itself by coming into the image of the divine pattern of Father and Son, we will find ourselves compelled to approach those in authority over us and appeal to them. Silence reveals both a lack of love for our authorities and also cowardice and an unwillingness to sacrifice for the truth's sake. Silence also causes us to partake of the guilt of the church's idolatry. For instance, if the Sabbath lesson promotes the Trinity, we need to prayerfully appeal to the pastor and the board that we can't find these things in the Bible and that we are appealing to them to consider what the Bible truly teaches on the subject.

I would hasten to add that the point of appeal for a wife of an unbelieving husband is her husband rather than the pastor of the church. If a wife of an unbelieving husband (meaning he believes in the Trinity) approaches the pastor then she shames her husband by her conduct and will certainly make things harder in reaching her husband.

In regard to making an appeal, I believe our Lord has placed before us a test of the heart. Are we willing to experience shame and contempt before our brethren for the sake of the Lord Jesus? If we are not willing to face scorn and derision now, how shall we stand when the Sunday Law comes to us? Those who walk through the door of appeal to their leaders will be strengthened to face the coming crisis over the Sabbath.

It is on this point that every man finds whether he has an anchor that holds the soul, "steadfast and sure while the billows roll." It is through the appeal process that we find whether we are "fastened to the rock which cannot move, grounded firm and deep in the Saviour's love."

I confess that appealing to my brethren placed me in places emotionally and mentally that tested my soul to the utmost limit. I learnt things about myself that I never would have known otherwise. As I look back on my appeal experience I can say, "Praise God for His mercy in revealing many things to me that needed changing in my life." Those who shortcut the appeal process may find the next level of testing too hard and may yield the faith. Oh I pray that this might not happen to any of us.

So once again, in conclusion, I state that the very knowledge we possess through the begotten Son formulates for us the divine pattern, which demands of us the need to appeal to our leaders and ask them to consider the truth that Jesus is the Son of the living God.

Once you have resolved to make an appeal I would encourage you to pray about who you should approach. Pick the authority figure in your life that you have the closest connection to and is the most likely to give you time to express your convictions. It may be your elder or an associate pastor; it may be your pastor, or it may be the conference president. As you pray the Lord will give you wisdom to know which direction to take.

Write out what you found from Scripture concerning the Son of God. You might consider including the statement about God from the Fundamental Principles found in the 1914 year book. See Appendix A at the back of the book. This statement was believed with "entire unanimity throughout the body" of Seventh-day Adventists at that time. If you were baptised before 1990, you might also present your baptismal vow which clearly presents Jesus as the Son of God. See Appendix B to see the difference before and after 1990. If you are remaining faithful to your baptismal vow, then gently enquire how the church can discipline you?

Place together the evidence as you see it and that has been most helpful to you. I would advise against simply handing someone else's material to the person in authority. It needs to be a personal appeal from your own heart. Once a leader expresses openness to study, then you might consider providing other materials. I might also add that any materials you would submit should come from sources that respect the divine pattern. If a leader should find material or hear speakers condemning the Adventist Church, your appeal is most certainly not going to be heard.

I raised the point earlier about motivation because making a Biblical appeal is all about trajectory. By trajectory we mean approaching your leader at the right angle as to give your appeal maximum impact. Get clear in your mind that you are submitting yourself and your research for the analysis of the person in authority. If in your trajectory reflects in any sense that you have come to show them the truth and that they need to submit to what you are saying, then you will miss your target. The divine pattern demands that we entreat as a son would entreat his father. We speak respectfully and with love. We need to be quick to listen and slow to speak. The aim of the appeal is to ask for help, to ask to be shown from the Scriptures where we might have made a mistake. We must be honest in this appeal and not assume that we are right and that no evidence could convince us otherwise. We must take whatever is given us to the Lord, pray about it and go back with our response.

When a leader perceives that you have studied this subject well, you may find he will then try to stall the process. This means facing long delays, missed meetings or a whole range of excuses that will surface. Let us remember that Satan is not keen on any appeals finding their mark and he will make it his business to stall the process and frustrate us in our appeal.

It is during this process that we might be accused of being stubborn, independent minded or divisive. It is at these times we need to remember Hannah when she was accused of being drunk by Eli. Let us, like her, reply "No, my lord," I am not drunk but in bitterness of soul for the Son of God.

During this time, you may observe that other church members start to withdraw their affection from you. You may experience a total shunning for making your appeal, but this is the path that those who love the Son of God often must walk.

Ask the Lord to grant you patience as you make your appeal. If you can't find any Scriptural reason to follow their suggestions, then appeal to them to discipline you as they see fit. At this point, if a leader feels he has enough authority to silence you, then he has the responsibility to discipline you. Any parent knows that to administer discipline to a child is something more painful to the parent than the child. If the minister has any of the Spirit of Christ in them, they will recoil from wanting to remove you from fellowship, but this is the price they must pay for their convictions that you are wrong and must be silent.

During this process we must refrain from the temptation to try and win others to our side. It is very tempting to act in a political manner and seek to bring other people to our point of view under the nose of the pastor. This shows a lack of respect and it also brings other people into controversy when they may not have yet had time to study the issue thoroughly.

Some people have the view that we must tell the members the truth. I assure you that nothing proclaims the truth more than your willingness to be deprived of privileges for the sake of what you believe. This speaks more for the truth than anything else. It may appear that this process yields no results but Heaven marks the faithfulness of those who have stood stiffly for the truth in the face of great opposition and possible scorn and derision.

Once you have been disciplined, then you are at liberty to share your beliefs with all who approach you within the church. If no one approaches you then you have nothing to say. Use whatever public forums are available to you where you are not in conflict with an authority figure that has leadership of that forum.

What about those who have already been disfellowshipped? As you recall events did you act in a respectful way? Is there anything you can recall that would require an apology for wrong actions or conduct? Take the time to write to those who you may feel you have offended and offer your apology. Then join in the work of praying for forgiveness on behalf of the church. It is my daily prayer that our Father in Heaven would forgive us as His people, and help our leaders and bless their families, and help as many as possible to find the light before it is too late.

This path is a narrow path, but one that I believe will prepare God's people to face the closing scenes of earth's history. Let us also remember that as we present the Son of God to our leaders, it is He who is on trial. Each time we appeal to the leaders of the church we are giving them the chance to vindicate the Son of God or condemn Him by your expulsion. The more people that are repelled in their appeals, the more the Son of God is rejected in the church. The more He is rejected, the more certain will come the judgements of God in response to the cries of His people to vindicate His Son and restore true authority in the church. The more that Christ is accepted in these appeals, the more certain will come the shaking of God's people. Either way the much needed change will come.

Friends, this current testing process although difficult, can also act as a gift from Heaven to burn self out of us. Few people welcome being scorned or deprived of fellowship for their faith, but those who drink this cup now with be strengthened to drink a greater draught in the Time of Jacob's Trouble.

10. Standing Alone

The process of appeal we described in the previous chapter raises the prospect of an individual standing alone for their convictions of the Word. It is not an easy thing for people to stand alone without the need for some kind of human support or encouragement. Such pressures can cause individuals to seek out others, seeking to win them to their understanding in order that they might gain the numbers before directly approaching existing leadership. Much evangelistic endeavour is motivated by people who come under conviction but do not have a foundation that allows them to stand alone. Such individuals will often be driven by the need for acceptance more than for the love of the truth. Standing alone does not need the support of anyone or anything outside the Word of God. Standing alone does not cause one to feel compelled to bring others to their understanding in order to no longer stand alone. Yet standing alone is not a natural human characteristic. Most of us are very vulnerable to the process called groupthink. What is groupthink?

> A mode of thinking that people engage in when they are deeply involved in a cohesive ingroup, when the members' strivings for unanimity override their motivation to realistically appraise alternative courses of action. (Janis, 1972). From *Wikipedia article* – Groupthink.

The human desire for belonging and acceptance has the capacity to cause people to override a proper process of investigation of the Word of God. If something is believed by the majority within a social group then the motivation to believe differently from that group must hold out for that person something of greater worth to them, something that is worth risking rejection by that group.

The pressure to conform to the wishes of the majority can cause leaders who know better to cave in. While Moses was in the mount receiving this instruction:

> **Exod 23:2** Thou shalt not follow a multitude to do evil; neither shalt thou speak in a cause to decline after many to wrest judgement:

Aaron was down below doing the exact opposite:

> **Exod 32:1-4** And when the people saw that Moses delayed to come down out of the mount, the people gathered themselves together unto Aaron, and said unto him, Up, make us gods, which shall go before us; for as for this Moses, the man that brought us up out of the land of Egypt, we wot not what is become of him. (2) And Aaron said unto them, Break off the golden earrings, which are in the ears of your wives, of your sons, and of your daughters, and bring them unto me. (3) And all the people brake off the golden earrings which were in their ears, and brought them unto Aaron. (4) And he received them at their hand, and fashioned it with a graving tool, after he had made it a molten calf: and they said, These be thy gods, O Israel, which brought thee up out of the land of Egypt.

Aaron feared the people more than he feared God, and in desiring their acceptance more than the truth, he caused Israel to sin.

> **Exod 32:21-22** And Moses said unto Aaron, What did this people unto thee, that thou hast brought so great a sin upon them? (22) And Aaron said, Let not the anger of my lord wax hot: thou knowest the people, that they are set on mischief.

Another man who feared the people was Saul:

> **1 Sam 15:24** And Saul said unto Samuel, I have sinned: for I have transgressed the commandment of the LORD, and thy words: because I feared the people, and obeyed their voice.

Rather than truly repent, he begged Samuel to come with him in order that the people would still honour him.

> **1 Sam 15:30** Then he said, I have sinned: yet honour
> me now, I pray thee, before the elders of my people, and
> before Israel, and turn again with me, that I may worship
> the LORD thy God.

In contrast to this we see the spirit of Joshua and Caleb when they gave their report of the Promised Land.

> **Num 14:6-10** And Joshua the son of Nun, and Caleb the
> son of Jephunneh, which were of them that searched the
> land, rent their clothes: (7) And they spake unto all the
> company of the children of Israel, saying, The land, which
> we passed through to search it, is an exceeding good land.
> (8) If the LORD delight in us, then he will bring us into
> this land, and give it us; a land which floweth with milk
> and honey. (9) Only rebel not ye against the LORD,
> neither fear ye the people of the land; for they are bread
> for us: their defence is departed from them, and the LORD
> is with us: fear them not. (10) But all the congregation
> bade stone them with stones. And the glory of the LORD
> appeared in the tabernacle of the congregation before all
> the children of Israel.

These men were willing to brave the majority opinion in order to state the facts. They were willing to risk their lives to stand for the truth.

Many of us may hold childhood scars from finding ourselves outside the favour of a group of children. I have a few experiences of being mocked and taunted for being different. As a young person, those experiences can be quite unsettling and can cause major shortcuts in thinking in order to be accepted. Parents often feel helpless as they watch their children become engulfed in a peer group that is going away from the teachings of the Word of God. The need for acceptance washes away the value that comes from standing for the truth.

Satan knows well the power of peer pressure and he uses it wherever he can to cause people to avoid reasoning from the Scriptures with a determination to search out the truth at all costs. Since we all live in this world, it is a certainty that at some point believing the truth will cost you the acceptance of a group you once belonged to. The Bible clearly tells us that it is impossible to believe the truth if we fear losing the honour of men:

> **John 5:44** How can ye believe, which receive honour one of another, and seek not the honour that cometh from God only?

Many people will be excluded from the kingdom of Heaven on this point alone. Notice what the Scripture says:

> **Rev 21:7-8** He that overcometh shall inherit all things; and I will be his God, and he shall be my son. (8) But the fearful, and unbelieving, and the abominable, and murderers, and whoremongers, and sorcerers, and idolaters, and all liars, shall have their part in the lake which burneth with fire and brimstone: which is the second death.

The first group mentioned amongst those who do not inherit all things of the Father are the fearful; those who were too afraid to face the majority opinion and risk losing their approval.

It is this human tendency that prevented many leaders who believed in Jesus from openly confessing him:

> **John 12:42-43** Nevertheless among the chief rulers also many believed on him; but because of the Pharisees they did not confess him, lest they should be put out of the synagogue: (43) For they loved the praise of men more than the praise of God.

Do we see a parallel today? Are there those who believe yet are fearful of being put out of the church for their belief in the Son of God?

The seed of the begotten Son that finds root in the receptive soul manifests itself in a willingness to face scorn, contempt and ridicule for the truth's sake. That seed we receive from Christ which He received from His Father and we can know the dimensions of the Seed in these words:

> **Matt 3:17** And lo a voice from heaven, saying, This is my beloved Son, in whom I am well pleased.

As Jesus rested in this assurance of His Father, He could face the angry mob, the murderous priests, the thuggish Roman guard and all the legions of hell. All this He could face knowing that His Father delighted in Him. The reward of following the truth is to receive the Spirit of truth which is the Spirit of Christ.

As we decide in our minds to love the begotten Son no matter what the cost, the Spirit of Jesus abides with us and we have our fellowship in the Father and the Son. I can say with absolute certainty that the joy and peace of their fellowship more than compensate for the loss of my former associates with their contempt and ridicule. The love of Jesus more than pays for the loss of my career, reputation and standing in the church; yea, I count these things as dung compared to the excellency of the knowledge of Jesus Christ my Lord.

Those who truly believe that Jesus is the Son of God will both find the strength to stand alone and the love to appeal to their church leaders with submissive grace.

Many times I questioned myself; I felt the pressure of the majority against me. I questioned, "what makes you so sure you are right, Adrian?" "There are virtually none in leadership who agree with you. Who do you think you are to take this stand?" Then I would go back to the Bible and read the plain testament concerning the Son of God. I would read again the many lines of evidence in the Bible and the Spirit of Prophecy. I would examine again the foundation our pioneers laid; I compared the testimony of the 1888 messengers; I poured over the *Review and Herald* articles and asked myself, "Are you sure, Adrian?" And the conviction came back stronger and more urgent than before. YES! YES! YES! I am sure that Jesus is the Son of the Father in truth and love, and no weapon fashioned against this confession will stand.

And with that conviction often came the sweet experience of peace—peace that I could never describe. I could feel the love of the Father for His Son IN me. As I embraced the truth of the Son of God, the realisation of the Father's love for me in Christ was beyond comprehension. Many times when I would receive a harsh email or a word from the wicked one to tempt me, my Saviour would send a word of encouragement to bless me. Often when I would walk, I would behold the sparrows and smile as I thought that I was of more value than many sparrows.

I can also testify that after I determined to confess the begotten Son before my brethren and not to be ashamed of His name by remaining silent, I found greater victory in my personal life. My thoughts and affections began to change at a faster rate. The things of the world that would attract me and divert me from my path grew strangely dim. Praise God for His sanctifying Spirit!

My friends, if you truly love the Son of the Father then you will love His remnant church. This love will compel you to confess the Lord Jesus before your church family, and the peace of Christ will give you the courage to stand alone without any political strategies or desires to draw away disciples to your position to create your own majority consensus. Willing to face whatever consequences may come, you will find yourself free to appeal to those in authority over you and to ask them to allow you to worship the Son of the living God within the Seventh-day Adventist Church. Choose the right because it is right and leave the consequences with God.

The Bible tells us:

> **John 8:32** And ye shall know the truth, and the truth shall make you free.

The truth sets us free from the fear of what others think of us; it sets us free from the need for acceptance from our peers. When we know that we are accepted by the Almighty Father through His Son, we need nothing else to sustain us.

If you wish to study more on this subject I would invite you to read my little book *Identity Wars*[1] that covers our true value in Christ in greater detail. It is through the principles of this little book that I found the peace to be able to stand alone in the eyes of men, yet to be standing with Christ and His angels.

---

[1] Go to www.identitywars.org.

Section 3. Consequences of Rejecting the Divine Pattern

11. Protection of Our Kinsman Redeemer

In chapter one, we noted the following:

> Apart from the direct blessings of joy, happiness and fellowship that flow to us through this divine pattern, there are also the protective blessings that we can accrue through the channel. In each case, the one "By Whom" things come, is under the protection and possesses the authority of the one "Of Whom" things come.

We see this principle of protection operating in the divine pattern with such Bible passages as:

> **Deut 32:11** As an eagle stirreth up her nest, fluttereth over her young, spreadeth abroad her wings, taketh them, beareth them on her wings:

> **Ruth 2:12** The LORD recompense thy work, and a full reward be given thee of the LORD God of Israel, under whose wings thou art come to trust.

The protection of "By Whom" agents occurs as they honour, respect and obey their "Of Whom" source. We see how Naomi instructed Ruth to place herself at Boaz's feet and then ask him to spread his skirt over her as a symbol of protection and provision.

> **Ruth 3:9** And he said, Who art thou? And she answered, I am Ruth thine handmaid: spread therefore thy skirt over thine handmaid; for thou art a near kinsman.

In lying at Boaz's feet, Ruth revealed the spirit of submission. She was inviting his protection and provision through the channel of blessing.

It is this principle of protection that will shield God's people during the time of trouble. We have seen that Psalm 91 has application to that time.[1] Let us consider parts of this Psalm and the protection given to God's people.

> **Psa 91:1-2** He that dwelleth in the secret place of the most High shall abide under the shadow of the Almighty. (2) I will say of the LORD, He is my refuge and my fortress: my God; in him will I trust.

As God's people come into line with the divine pattern of submission through His delegated agencies, they find themselves coming under His shadow of protection. This is the secret place of all those who put their trust in Him.

> **Psa 91:3-4** Surely he shall deliver thee from the snare of the fowler, and from the noisome pestilence. (4) He shall cover thee with his feathers, and under his wings shalt thou trust: his truth shall be thy shield and buckler.

The earth will soon be swept with disease, natural disasters and the violence of men. Many people's hearts will fail for fear of these things coming on the earth. Only those who know the God of Israel and His Son will receive the protection of the Almighty.

> I saw that Satan was at work in these ways to distract, deceive, and draw away God's people, just now in this sealing time. I saw some who were not standing stiffly for present truth. Their knees were trembling, and their feet sliding, because they were not firmly planted on the truth, and the covering

---

[1] "Thus God will destroy the wicked from off the earth. But the righteous will be preserved in the midst of these commotions, as Noah was preserved in the ark. God will be their refuge, and under His wings shall they trust. Says the psalmist: 'Because thou hast made the Lord, which is my refuge, even the Most High, thy habitation; there shall no evil befall thee.' Psalm 91:9, 10. 'In the time of trouble He shall hide me in His pavilion: in the secret of His tabernacle shall He hide me.' Psalm 27:5. God's promise is, 'Because he hath set his love upon Me, therefore will I deliver him: I will set him on high, because he hath known My name.'" Psalm 91:14. *Patriarchs and Prophets*, page 110.

of Almighty God could not be drawn over them while they were thus trembling. Satan was trying his every art to hold them where they were, until the sealing was past, until the covering was drawn over God's people, and they left without a shelter from the burning wrath of God, in the seven last plagues. God has begun to draw this covering over His people, and it will soon be drawn over all who are to have a shelter in the day of slaughter. *Early Writings*, page 44.

We recall how the Jewish leaders in the time of Christ refused to believe on the Son of God. Because of their refusal to accept Him, they refused His protection and provision and were left to the mercy of Rome.

Matt 23:37 O Jerusalem, Jerusalem, thou that killest the prophets, and stonest them which are sent unto thee, how often would I have gathered thy children together, even as a hen gathereth her chickens under her wings, and ye would not!

Let me state it clearly so that none will misunderstand:

The protection and provision of God both now and in the crisis just ahead will only be given to those who reverence His Son. He that hath the Son, hath life.

The issue of whether we believe Jesus is truly the Son of God involves the question of protection and provision. This is not simply an academic discussion of theological disagreement. If we place ourselves under the banner of a being that God has not explicitly revealed to us in Scripture then we are placing ourselves outside of God's protection and provision. A rejection of God's Son is an automatic invitation for the wicked one to confuse our thinking, twist our minds, invade our homes, entice us to a myriad of temptations and ultimately to end our lives. A rejection of the Son of God has invited Rome to invade us and control many of our activities as a church.

Our Lord Jesus, strong man of the house of Adventism, has been bound by Satan through the teachings of the Trinity within our church. He has now entered the house and is spoiling the members of the house.

Matt 12:29 Or else how can one enter into a strong man's house, and spoil his goods, except he first bind the strong man? and then he will spoil his house.

In this verse Jesus speaks to the principle of protection and provision. In this case the situation is reversed where Satan is the strong man or protector/enslaver and he is the one that needs binding to release those under his control.

With the release of the 1980 Fundamental statement concerning God, the Adventist Church stepped out from the direct protection and provision of the God of Israel. It is since this time that we have seen many events rock the church. One event that sticks clearly in my mind as an Australian is the night I heard that Lindy Chamberlain was convicted of murdering her baby daughter and their appeal that a dingo had taken the child was rejected. As a 14-year-old boy I looked into the heavens and wondered, "Where are you God? Why have you let this happen?" Is there any connection between the rejection of God's Son and His ability to protect His people?

It was also around this time that a landslide of ministers rejected the Most Holy Place ministry of our Lord Jesus. This disaster had been building for the decade before the 1980's even as the move to install the Trinitarian god upon the throne of Adventism. Yet this disaster did not fall upon us until after our church confessed this false god. What about the strange financial dealings that arose at this time as well as the open attack on Ellen White? Is there any connection between these events? Do we see that a layer of protection was stripped away from our church when we accepted the Trinity formally in 1980?

It was not long after 1980 that certain doors started opening for evangelism in various communication mediums. Are we sure that the miracles that started to occur at this time have a Heavenly source? Could Satan be allowed to work miracles for Adventists to convince them that God was still leading them when it was Satan himself that was now the leader? Have the very elect been deceived through these miracles that have placed "Adventist Programs" in millions of homes around the world? Why is it that when large sums of money are donated for projects that few people would ever question whether Satan would invest in Adventist programs once they had left the protection of the God of Israel? We have been warned:

> Some declare their unbelief in the work that the Lord has given me to do because, as they say, "Mrs. E. G. White works no miracles." **But those who look for miracles as a sign of divine guidance are in grave danger of deception.** It

is stated in the Word that **the enemy will work through his agents who have departed from the faith**, and they will seemingly work miracles, even to the bringing down of fire out of heaven in the sight of men. By means of "lying wonders" Satan would deceive, if possible, the very elect. *Selected Messages, Volume 2*, page 53.

Could some of these miracles involve money and "providential events"? Could Satan be allowed to do these things if we have departed from the faith by the introduction of the 27 Fundamentals?

As we recall the experience of Israel that we are repeating, I believe there are many lessons for us.

> **Num 21:5-6** And the people spake against God, and against Moses, Wherefore have ye brought us up out of Egypt to die in the wilderness? for there is no bread, neither is there any water; and our soul loatheth this light bread. (6) And the LORD sent fiery serpents among the people, and they bit the people; and much people of Israel died.

> If with all these tokens of His love the people still continued to complain, the Lord would withdraw His protection until they should be led to appreciate His merciful care, and return to Him with repentance and humiliation. **Because they had been shielded by divine power they had not realized the countless dangers by which they were continually surrounded.** In their ingratitude and unbelief they had anticipated death, and now the Lord permitted death to come upon them. The poisonous serpents that infested the wilderness were called fiery serpents, on account of the terrible effects produced by their sting, it causing violent inflammation and speedy death. As the protecting hand of God was removed from Israel, great numbers of the people were attacked by these venomous creatures. *Patriarchs and Prophets*, page 429.

Our God has given Adventism many tokens of His love and grace. He protected us from many of Satan's attacks. But our people began to desire to be like the other Protestant churches; many wanted to be educated like people in the world; we sought the accreditation standards of the world; we wearied of the 1888 teachings that Jesus truly was the Son of God and the Son of Man who took our flesh. Many of our people despised the health message and standards that were given us as a people and so when our church bowed before the

Trinity god in 1980, Adventism stepped out from under the protection of the God of Israel.

Friends, I believe it is only the pleading of Jesus before His Father that has prevented many of our people from being swept away by Satan. Our Saviour knows that many of us in confusion bowed unknowingly before Baal. How many of us should have lost our lives in the last 30 year period? How much thanks and gratitude do we owe our Father for His long suffering and patience with our foolishness?

> **Num 21:7** Therefore the people came to Moses, and said, We have sinned, for we have spoken against the LORD, and against thee; pray unto the LORD, that he take away the serpents from us. And Moses prayed for the people.

Dear Father, I pause to thank you for your mercy, your sweet mercy in not allowing us to be destroyed by the serpents that have come into our camp. I know that many have been bitten and are wounded; many have watched their children, family and friends succumb to the poison of the wicked one and turn their backs on the crucified Son of God. Oh Father, please forgive us and help us and heal us. Turn our hearts back to you and help us to see clearly the path that we must walk. We plead these things in Jesus' name.

Friends, I wondered for years why some of our leaders were letting so many evils come into our church and would seem to do nothing about it. Can we see that in accepting the Trinity that God withheld His ability to guide our pastor's minds? Our leaders become exposed to doctrines of devils, and they lose their ability to discern when Satan is stealing in upon us? Can we see that Satan has greater power to deceive our leaders because of the Trinity and as he deceives them, he then turns to those under their care and shows some of them what he is doing, so they will rise up in anger against the leaders? We need to pray for our leaders that they will turn and look upon the Son of Man who was lifted up and be healed of their blindness. I confess I was blind for so long. I am ashamed to say that I believed in the Trinity; I was reading so much Bible and Spirit of Prophecy and I just could not see that I was worshipping Baal.

I tried so hard to overcome my youthful desires for sports and appetite. I tried keeping my mind pure, but without the protection of the Son of God within the context of the divine pattern, Satan just kept attacking me and his power over me was great; I would go into waves of despair and just feel I was never going to be saved.

It is on these issues that many Adventist pastors have been driven out of the Most Holy Place and have given up a belief that God's people will stand without an Intercessor at the end of time. They start preaching, "We will sin until Jesus comes" and all the people who are groaning under Seventh-day Adventist standards feel they are being set free from legalism, when all they have done is retreated to the Holy Place where they can be breathed upon by Satan who pretends to minister there as Christ.

I confess that in coming back to the belief that Jesus is the Son of God, our family encountered a battering. Since I had bowed the knee to Baal as a Seventh-day Adventist minister, Satan was allowed to buffet me and my family for a period of time. This may happen for others as well, but our Father only allows these things for our character; to learn to trust Him and to realise that every day we have peace is only because of the mercy of God. Each day that I am able to write, I know I have the protection of our Father. I wish to thank many of you as readers who I know are praying. I don't take these things for granted, and I raise my heart in praise and thanksgiving for our Father's mercy and protection through Jesus – the Son of the living God.

I just need to pause again and think about our mighty Saviour, Michael, Captain of the Lord's host. *Oh Lord Jesus, I throw myself at Your feet and I plead with You to throw Your skirt over my nakedness and take me into Your care and protection. I know that I have sinned against Heaven and earth and am no longer worthy to be called by Your name, but I rest in the assurance of Your Word.*

> **1 John 1:9** If we confess our sins, he is faithful and just to forgive us our sins, and to cleanse us from all unrighteousness.

> **John 6:37** All that the Father giveth me shall come to me; and him that cometh to me I will in no wise cast out.

Dear Father, please send the Spirit of Your Son to protect us and our families. Please protect our leaders who are confused and blinded to the truth of Your Son. Please send Your angels to help them and bless them and show them the things You are showing us. We are no better than they are. We have sinned and worshipped Baal and are worthy of death even as they are. How I plead with You to speak to my fellow pastors. Lord Jesus I feel Your love for them in my heart and I thank You for sharing this with me. Please Father, open the eyes of our leaders, we petition You to encourage them to let us worship Your Son in the church that You established. Please erect the pole once again that we may gaze upon the Son of Man who was broken for us and truly died on Calvary, not just slept. Oh Father forgive us for degrading the atoning sacrifice of Your Son and turning away from You. As Daniel prayed:

Dan 9:8-18[2] O Lord, to us belongeth confusion of face, to our kings, to our princes, and to our fathers, because we have sinned against thee. (9) To the Lord our God belong mercies and forgivenesses, though we have rebelled against him; (10) Neither have we obeyed the voice of the LORD our God, to walk in his laws, which he set before us by his servants the prophets. (11) Yea, all Israel have transgressed thy law, even by departing, that they might not obey thy voice; therefore the curse is poured upon us, and the oath that is written in the law of Moses the servant of God, because we have sinned against him. (12) And he hath confirmed his words, which he spake against us, and against our judges that judged us, by bringing upon us a great evil: for under the whole heaven hath not been done as hath been done upon Jerusalem. (13) As it is written in the law of Moses, all this evil is come upon us: yet made we not our prayer before the LORD our God, that we might turn from our iniquities, and understand thy truth. (14) Therefore hath the LORD watched upon the evil, and brought it upon us: for the LORD our God is righteous in all his works which he doeth: for we obeyed not his voice. (15) And now, O Lord our God, that hast brought thy people forth out of the land of Egypt with a mighty hand, and hast gotten thee renown, as at this day; we have sinned, we have done wickedly. (16) O Lord, according to all thy righteousness, I beseech thee, let thine anger and thy fury be turned away from thy city Jerusalem [church Adventism], thy holy mountain [channel of blessing]: because for our sins, and for the iniquities of our fathers, Jerusalem and thy people are become a reproach to all that are about us. (17) Now therefore, O our God, hear the prayer of thy servant,

---

[2] Comments in square brackets supplied.

and his supplications, and cause thy face to shine upon thy sanctuary that is desolate [through the rejection of true Son of God, our priest], for the Lord's sake. (18) O my God, incline thine ear, and hear; open thine eyes, and behold our desolations, and the city which is called by thy name: for we do not present our supplications before thee for our righteousnesses, but for thy great mercies.

Friends, it is my prayer that you will join Daniel's prayer knowing that our leaders have been blinded because of a loss of protection from Heaven. God has allowed a curse to fall upon our leaders so that the "chief men; the mighty men of old" like our pioneers, have been taken away.[3] Let us pray that the leaders who have not yet determined to fight the truth about the Son of God will yet turn to Him and find protection.

Let us pray that the spirit of Ruth will return to our leaders and that they will go and fall before the feet of our Kinsman Redeemer and plead for Him to place His protecting skirt over the nakedness of Seventh-day Adventism.

---

[3] See Isa 3:1,2. See also my sermon "The Downward Path." vimeo.com/15830874.

12. Samson's Blindness

The Bible tells us that hair is not just a practical covering but also a symbol of being under authority.

> **1 Cor 11:15** But if a woman have long hair, it is a glory to her: for her hair is given her for a covering.

> **1 Cor 11:10** (RV) for this cause ought the woman to have a sign of authority on her head, because of the angels.

If we look carefully at the symbolism attached to hair we notice something interesting. We see that men in Bible times had long hair hanging from their faces and women had long hair upon their heads. Through the symbolism of hair we see that blessing flows from the male to the female.

> **Psa 133:2** It is like the precious ointment upon the head, that ran down upon the beard, even Aaron's beard: that went down to the skirts of his garments;

We see in the above verse the symbol of oil running down the beard as a symbol of the Spirit. Notice also that it ran down to his skirt, the symbol of protection. A woman's long hair is a symbol of being in submission to the channel of blessing and receiving the Spirit of God upon them. A woman's long and flowing hair is symbolic of her being strengthened by the Spirit through her submission to her husband.

In most cases if men had long hair, it was a shame to them because they represented the "Of Whom" component of the blessing system.

> **1 Cor 11:14** Doth not even nature itself teach you, that, if a man have long hair, it is a shame unto him?

Yet in certain cases some men had long hair, as in the Nazarite vow, where a man did not cut his hair. In such cases these men were under special direction of the Holy Spirit and had a special work to do.

It is significant that Jesus had long hair but also a beard. We see in Christ both aspects of the divine blessing, both upon His head from His Father and coming forth from His mouth as reflected in the beard.

> His hair was white and curly and lay on His shoulders. *Early Writings*, page 16.

> They then took the reed from His hand and smote Him with it upon the head, causing the thorns to penetrate His temples, sending the blood trickling down His face and beard. *Early Writings*, page 170.

The long hair of Christ was a symbol of the special submissive relationship He sustained to the Father and the blessing of the Holy Spirit that fell upon Him from His Father.

> **Matt 3:16** And Jesus, when he was baptized, went up straightway out of the water: and, lo, the heavens were opened unto him, and he saw the Spirit of God descending like a dove, and lighting upon him.

Empowered and protected by the Spirit of the Father, Jesus then spoke with authority.[1]

> **John 3:34-35** For he whom God hath sent speaketh the words of God: for God giveth not the Spirit by measure unto him. (35) The Father loveth the Son, and hath given all things into his hand.

---

[1] "Never before had angels listened to such a prayer as Christ offered at His baptism, and they were solicitous to be the bearers of the message from the Father to His Son. But, no! direct from the Father issues the light of His glory. The heavens were opened, and beams of glory rested upon the Son of God and assumed the form of a dove, in appearance like burnished gold. The dove-like form was emblematical of the meekness and gentleness of Christ. While the people stood spell-bound with amazement, their eyes fastened upon Christ, from the opening heavens came these words: "This is My beloved Son, in whom I am well pleased." The words of confirmation that Christ is the Son of God were given to inspire faith in those who witnessed the scene, and to sustain the Son of God in His arduous work. Notwithstanding the Son of God was clothed with humanity, yet Jehovah, with His own voice, assures Him of His Sonship with the Eternal. In this manifestation to His Son, God accepts humanity as exalted through the excellence of His beloved Son." *Review and Herald*, January 21, 1873

John 6:63 It is the spirit that quickeneth; the flesh profiteth nothing: the words that I speak unto you, they are spirit, and they are life.

It is with these thoughts in mind that we turn to the story of Samson.[2] This man was a Nazarite and was told not to cut his hair.

Judges 13:5 For, lo, thou shalt conceive, and bear a son; and no razor shall come on his head: for the child shall be a Nazarite unto God from the womb: and he shall begin to deliver Israel out of the hand of the Philistines.

The long hair of Samson symbolised the Spirit of God that was given him to possess supernatural strength.

In finding the way into the Most Holy Place in Heaven, Adventism received an endowment of the Spirit that would enable them to keep all the commandments of God. They were to receive supernatural strength to preach the Third Angel's Message and then face the Time of Jacob's Trouble without a mediator.

There I beheld Jesus, a great High Priest, standing before the Father. On the hem of His garment was a bell and a pomegranate, a bell and a pomegranate. **Those who rose up with Jesus would send up their faith to Him in the holiest, and pray,** "My Father, give us Thy Spirit." Then Jesus would breathe upon them the Holy Ghost. **In that breath was light, power, and much love, joy, and peace.** *Early Writings,* page 55.

The problem for Samson was that he loved women that were from the Philistines.

Judges 14:1-2 And Samson went down to Timnath, and saw a woman in Timnath of the daughters of the Philistines. (2) And he came up, and told his father and his mother, and said, I have seen a woman in Timnath of the daughters of the Philistines: now therefore get her for me to wife.

Adventism began to mingle with other Protestants after 1888, and men arose within our ranks that desired to be more closely connected

---

[2] "The Bible has accumulated and bound up together its treasures for this last generation. All the great events and solemn transactions of Old Testament history have been, and are, repeating themselves in the church in these last days." 7 *Manuscript Release,* page 417

to them. As Leroy Froom[3] wrote to the then President concerning the meetings with Martin and Barnhouse[4] :

> I do not know where all this will lead but we do know we have won friends in a powerful circle – friends who believe we have been unjustly treated. Leroy Froom to R.R. Figuhr, Apr 26, 1955.

Just as Leroy Froom did not know where all these meetings with Barnhouse and Martin would lead, so Samson had no idea where his liaisons with Delilah would lead.

The secret of Samson's strength was in his hair, and the secret of Adventism's strength was in its knowledge of Daniel 8:14 that opened a door into the Most Holy Place and allowed us to receive the true power of the Holy Spirit.

As Samson foolishly yielded his secret to Delilah who was hired by the Philistines, so Adventism yielded her strength by altering many things that showed us the way into the Most Holy Place. Most notably was the switching of the God we worshipped. Notice carefully the confession found in *Questions on Doctrine*, page 21.

> In Common with Conservative Christians and the Historic Protestant Creeds, We Believe.
>
> 1. That God is the Sovereign Creator, upholder

---

[3] Leroy Edwin Froom (1890-1974) was a highly influential Adventist minister and Theologian. He played a central role in Adventist discussions with representatives from other Protestant denominations. His historical work called Conditionalist Faith of our Fathers reveals his devotion to Athanasius and the Trinity. "ATHANASIUS (c. 297-373), bishop of Alexandria and most prominent theologian of the fourth century, is commonly called the "defender of orthodoxy," **because of his conspicuous championship of the eternal deity of Christ** in the battle over the Godhead, as against the prolonged attacks of Arianism." *Conditionalist Faith of our Fathers Vol 1* Page 1061

[4] The publication of *Questions on Doctrine* grew out of a series of conferences between a few Adventist spokepersons and Protestant representatives from 1955 to 1956. The roots of this conference originated in a series of dialogues between Pennsylvania conference president, T. E. Unruh, and evangelical Bible teacher and magazine editor Donald Grey Barnhouse. Unruh was particularly concerned because of a scathing review written by Barnhouse about Ellen White's book, *Steps to Christ*. Unruh had sent him a copy of the book in 1949. In the spring of 1955 Barnhouse commissioned Walter Martin to write a book about Seventh-day Adventists. Martin requested a meeting with Adventist leaders so that he could question them about their beliefs. – Wikipedia, http://en.wikipedia.org/wiki/Questions_on_Doctrine

and ruler of the universe, and that He is eternal, omnipotent, omniscient, and omnipresent.

2. That the Godhead, the Trinity, comprises God the Father, Christ the Son, and the Holy Spirit.

Leroy Froom played a key role in preparing the book *Questions on Doctrine*. He certainly was in agreement with historical Protestant creeds. Notice these statements from him:

> May I here make **a frank personal confession**? When, back between 1926 and 1928, I was asked by our leaders to give a series of **studies on the Holy Spirit**, covering the North American union ministerial institutes of 1928, I found that, aside from priceless leads found in the Spirit of Prophecy, **there was practically nothing in our literature** setting forth a sound Biblical exposition in this tremendous field of study. There were no previous pathfinding books on the question in our literature. Leroy Edwin Froom, *Movement of Destiny*, page 322 (1971).

> **I was compelled to search out a score of valuable books written by men outside of our faith**— . . . men like Murray, Simpson, Gordon, Holden, Meyer, McNeill, Moody, Waugh, McConkey, Scroggie, Howden, Smith, McKensie, McIntosh, Brooks, Dixon, Kyle, Morgan, Needham, Pierson, Seiss, Thomas, West, and a score of others—for initial clues and suggestions, and to open up beckoning vistas to intensive personal study. Having these, I went on from there. But they were decided early helps. And **scores, if not hundreds, could confirm the same sobering conviction that some of these other men frequently had a deeper insight into the spiritual things of God than many of our own men then had on the Holy Spirit and the triumphant life.** It was still a largely obscure theme. Leroy Edwin Froom, *Movement of Destiny*, page 324

How is it that men from churches that had refused to go into the Most Holy Place by faith with Jesus in 1844, could receive deeper spiritual insights into the things of God than those who were reaching into the Most Holy Place? Did not the prophet tell us what spirit was coming to those who rejected the work of Jesus in the Most Holy place?

I turned to look at the company who were still bowed before the throne; they did not know that Jesus had left it. Satan appeared to be by the throne, trying to carry on the work of God. I saw them look up to the throne, and pray, "Father, give us Thy Spirit." **Satan would then breathe upon them an unholy influence; in it there was light and much power, but no sweet love, joy, and peace.** Satan's object was to keep them deceived and to draw back and deceive God's children. *Early Writings*, page 56.

By expressing a belief in God that was in common with conservative Protestant creeds, Adventism altered her whole understanding of the mediatorial work of Christ. This was not understood at first as these changes were foundational, not on the surface, but well down and hidden from view. The one thing that was noticed was the shift in emphasis on the atonement in the Most Holy Place. M. L. Andreasen[5] cried aloud through his *Letters to the Churches*. His warning was valid though he also was on the same shifting sand as his brethren in regard to the Trinity. Both Froom and Andreasen played a role in causing many Adventists to retreat from the Most Holy Place. The 'final generation' theology of Andreasen, devoid of an 1888 understanding of the mediatorial work of Christ, led to a conservative movement in Adventism that preached high standards yet without the knowledge of a mediator that had inherited all things from His Father.[6] (See my presentation – "The Heart of the 1888 Message"). The spirit of this movement has often been aggressive, strident and almost boxer-like. The lack of this knowledge skewed the understanding of righteousness by faith and caused despair for many Adventists. After the push by the conservatives, a counter balance movement spearheaded by several Adventist scholars armed with Froom's 'completed atonement at the cross' emphasis, opened the door back to the Holy Place and scratched the itching ears of poor Adventist saints weary of Andreasen's 'final generation.' These

[5] "M.[ilian] L.[auritz] Andreasen (1876–1962), was a Seventh-day Adventist theologian, pastor and author. He was one of the church's most prominent and influential theologians during the 1930s and 1940s. Andreasen promoted the teaching known popularly as Last Generation Theology, controversial for its views on atonement and salvation. Andreasen became well known for his protests against Adventist church leaders during the last years of his life." - Wikipedia

[6] See my presentation – "The Heart of the 1888 Message" http://vimeo.com/20699949

scholars spoke with the mouth of the fiery serpents they had been stung with.

The book *Questions On Doctrine* is the symbolic scissors in the hands of Delilah that took Adventism's strength[7] and set the path for Adventism's eyes to be gouged out with the 1980 Fundamental confession. It was at the time of this confession that the Philistines cried for joy that they had now mastered Adventism.

All of Samson's training, standards and good living were swallowed up through his desire for union with strange women. So too, Adventism's training and high calling were swept aside by its desire for the daughters of Babylon.

The confession of faith that claimed we stood in common with Conservative Protestant creeds was a firm declaration that, "We will not have this man to reign over us" (Luke 19:14).[8] The dear Son of God was shown the door with the printing and circulation of *Questions on Doctrine*. With the rejection of Christ, our educational institutions were swept with fiery serpents infected with higher criticism, modern methods of writing history and the scientific methods consistent with evolutional theory. A *Newsweek* magazine article from 1971 documents accurately how Adventism was swept by demonic forces. Quoting Dr Pipim's analysis of the article:

> **Strategy to Change Adventism**. But the article also proceeded to mention a startling development in the church. The magazine highlighted the efforts by "liberals in the SDA church, who would like to recover

---

[7] Jer 7:28-29 But thou shalt say unto them, This is a nation that obeyeth not the voice of the LORD their God, nor receiveth correction: truth is perished, and is cut off from their mouth. (29) Cut off thine hair, O Jerusalem, and cast it away, and take up a lamentation on high places; for the LORD hath rejected and forsaken the generation of his wrath.

[8] "History is being repeated. In our day we meet the same false reasoning among the rulers and the ministers as the people met when Christ was upon the earth. We need to consider the words of Christ. "Take heed that no man deceive you." The Jews were deceiving themselves. It was not because of a lack of light and evidence that Christ was not received, and believed, and honored as the Messiah; it was the malignity and jealousy and prejudice that bound so large a number with its cruel power. Minds clouded with prejudice, warped with envy and unholy passion, will not come to the word of God for their decision. Those who sat in Moses' seat instilled into the minds of the people their false interpretations of Scripture." *Signs of the Times* July 23, 1896

the early Adventist tradition of dissent." According to the liberals "**you will find few seminary professors who admit to the 6,000 year theory, and many Adventists no longer believe that the days of Creation were each 24 hours long**." The liberals also charge that "Adventists traditionally have placed too literal an interpretation on the second coming— thinking it was just around the corner--and failed to recognize the power of that doctrine to motivate Christians to change the world around them." And at a time when Adventists were expected to show great interest in end-time events (known technically as apocalyptic eschatology), in the opinion of the liberal Adventist scholars the church was "fatally afflicted with eschatological paranoia."

Significantly, the Newsweek article also stated the **strategy of liberal Adventism to reinterpret the church's historic doctrines on creation, the second-coming, and last day events: "As a first step toward recovering the dissenting spirit of the past, liberal Adventists contend, the church ought to rid itself of dependence upon an exaggerated Biblical literalism**." Samuel Pipim, *Receiving the Word*, page 75.[9]

The biggest serpent of all to bite Adventism is revealed in this desire to "rid itself of dependence upon an exaggerated Biblical literalism." In the rejection of a literal Son of a literal Father, our church turned first to the metaphorical Father and Son which in turn opened to the now drunken church a whole system of intellectual philosophy. Down went the literal Sanctuary; the literal Son of Man who took our nature; the literal male pastor; for many, the literal six day week; the literal victory over sin; these and many other doctrines were swept aside in drunken blindness.[10] So true are the words of Leroy Froom that he knew not where all this would lead!

One of the evidences of this blindness that came upon us is the confession of the then General Conference President concerning the introduction of the new Fundamental Beliefs:

---

[9] Italics in original.

[10] See my sermon "The Inroads of Spiritualism." http://vimeo.com/15862381. See also chapter 25 of my book *The Return of Elijah*. Available from Amazon.com.

So it is important that we look at this statement carefully and that when we have finished looking, **we know that we have not done violence, that we have not allowed anything to become eroded or weakened**, but rather that we have strengthened and helped, and perhaps become more lucid and clear.

We are not suggesting changing any belief or doctrine that this church has held. We have no interest in tearing up any of the foundations of historical Adventism. This document is not designed to do that, nor to open the way so that it can be done. It should be clear that we are not adding anything nor are we deleting anything in terms of historical Adventist theology. We are trying to express our beliefs in a way that will be understood today. N.C. Wilson, *Review and Herald*, April 23, 1980.

I am certain that our President at that time fully meant what he said. He did not believe that the church was changing anything. Yet having rejected the protection of the true Son of God in the release of the *Questions on Doctrine* confession that was in common with Conservative Protestant creeds, we can only feel sorry for any man that has been blinded by the metaphorical fog that comes with such Trinitarian confessions. I am in no way condemning our President. I was just as blinded as he was. I would not dare cast a stone at him, yet these are the facts of history, and proper remedy only comes from proper diagnosis.

As a testament to this blindness that told us we were not changing anything, we heard the now famous assessment 13 years later in the words:

> Most of the founders of Seventh-day Adventism would not be able to join the church today if they had to subscribe to the denomination's Fundamental Beliefs. More specifically, most would not be able to agree to belief number 2, which deals with the doctrine of the trinity. George Knight, *Ministry*, October 1993, page 10.

If we were not changing anything and we were not tearing up the historical foundations of Adventism, then why would our pioneers no longer be able to join the church? Many people have suggested that this was just a lie to hide a deeper agenda. Can you accuse a blind drunk man of lying? It would be hard to get such a confession to stand in court.

So now Adventism is grinding out corn for the Philistines and feeding their kingdom rather than the kingdom of Heaven. Some of us have come to our senses after years of living with no strength, no eyes and no hair!

Who is the little child that will lead Adventism to the secret of Babylon's power; this child of the Philistines that leads Adventism to the pillars of Babylon to smash them? These are things to ponder as we lament the blindness of Adventism. Who was the Eli of Adventism who went blind to the work that was happening in the 1940's and 1950's and let their sons Hophni (boxer) and Phinehas (mouth of the serpent) take the ark out of the Most Holy Place? These are all things we can ponder and pray about.

Apart from seeking to lay before you lines of thought that give context to our present situation, I am also appealing to you to be kind to leaders in the Adventist Church, many of whom are drunk with wine, bitten by fiery serpents, full of poison as well as suffering blindness and baldness.

Let us also remember that many groups that have arisen in Adventism, professing a belief in the begotten Son, have descended from the same history and have become blinded to the divine pattern and, in their pain from the serpents, have thrown off their allegiance to God's remnant church. Let us try to be patient with each other as we try to detoxify from the serpent's venom we all inherited.

It is only the mercies of our God that have allowed some of us to become semi-coherent. Some of us have been granted to see men as trees walking. Let us cry to the Son of David to have mercy on all of us and to give us back our vision, for indeed there is no open vision in the land. 1 Sam 3:1.

Let us remember the story of Jesus in Matthew 20. There were two blind men:

> **Matt 20:30** And, behold, two blind men sitting by the way side, when they heard that Jesus passed by, cried out, saying, Have mercy on us, O Lord, thou Son of David.

One of the blind men is the church who has rejected the Son of God and forsaken our divine "Of Whom" husband. The other blind man represents those who have rejected His beloved Church; the "By Whom" channel to whom Christ is betrothed. We both need to ask the Saviour:

> **Matt 20:32-34** And Jesus stood still, and called them, and said, What will ye that I shall do unto you? (33) They say unto him, Lord, that our eyes may be opened. (34) So Jesus had compassion on them, and touched their eyes: and immediately their eyes received sight, and they followed him.

May Jesus have compassion on all of us for our blindness, a blindness that came because we rejected the protection and provisions of our Kinsman Redeemer. We refused to have His skirt over us.

Let our prayer be: "Lord, that our eyes may be opened."

Section 4. Receiving Blessing Through a Corrupt Channel

13. Hannah's Sterling Example

With the history we have considered in the previous chapter revealing the metaphorical fog that has led our church into apostasy, it is natural for many to assume that there is no blessing in looking to the leaders of the Seventh-day Adventist Church. Yet I believe that there are lessons for us in the story of Hannah that apply to our current situation.

In the first chapter of Samuel we have the case of Hannah who was struggling under the weight of being childless, and beyond this she had to face the scornful words of another wife who could boast of producing children while she apparently could not.

> **1 Sam 1:1,2** Now there was a certain man of Ramathaimzophim, of mount Ephraim, and his name was Elkanah, the son of Jeroham, the son of Elihu, the son of Tohu, the son of Zuph, an Ephrathite: And he had two wives; the name of the one was Hannah, and the name of the other Peninnah: and Peninnah had children, but Hannah had no children.

> **1 Sam 1:4-7** And when the time was that Elkanah offered, he gave to Peninnah his wife, and to all her sons and her daughters, portions: (5) But unto Hannah he gave a worthy portion; for he loved Hannah: but the LORD had shut up her womb. (6) And her adversary also provoked her sore, for to make her fret, because the LORD had shut

up her womb. (7) And as he did so year by year, when she went up to the house of the LORD, so she provoked her; therefore she wept, and did not eat.

Hannah's husband Elkanah did not appear to understand his priestly role to pray for his wife as Isaac did for Rebekah:

Gen 25:21 And Isaac entreated the LORD for his wife, because she was barren: and the LORD was entreated of him, and Rebekah his wife conceived.

Instead he unwittingly bruised her further by trying to comfort her with the words, "Am I not better to you than ten sons?"

Hannah did not respond to her husband like Rachel did to Jacob when she was in a similar situation.

Gen 30:1 And when Rachel saw that she bare Jacob no children, Rachel envied her sister; and said unto Jacob, Give me children, or else I die.

The trial that Hannah endured having to compete with another woman and having no child made life almost unbearable, but rather than vent her frustrations, she took them to the Lord.[1]

1 Sam 1:10 And she was in bitterness of soul, and prayed unto the LORD, and wept sore.

If this was not enough, when she was in the temple praying she was charged by the High Priest with being a drunkard.

1 Sam 1:12-13 And it came to pass, as she continued praying before the LORD, that Eli marked her mouth. (13) Now Hannah, she spake in her heart; only her lips moved, but her voice was not heard: therefore Eli thought she had been drunken.

Let us consider this point of the story very carefully. Hannah's lot was made very hard because of her circumstances; she was scorned by

---

[1] Her husband vainly sought to comfort her. "Why weepest thou? and why eatest thou not? and why is thy heart grieved?" he said; "am I not better to thee than ten sons?" Hannah uttered no reproach. The burden which she could share with no earthly friend she cast upon God. Earnestly she pleaded that He would take away her reproach and grant her the precious gift of a son to nurture and train for Him. And she made a solemn vow that if her request were granted, she would dedicate her child to God, even from its birth. *Patriarchs and Prophets*, Page 569.

a rival wife and not understood by her husband. Add to this the fact that Eli was not a faithful priest.

> Eli was priest and judge in Israel. He held the highest and most responsible positions among the people of God. As a man divinely chosen for the sacred duties of the priesthood, and set over the land as the highest judicial authority, he was looked up to as an example, and he wielded a great influence over the tribes of Israel. But although he had been appointed to govern the people, he did not rule his own household. Eli was an indulgent father. Loving peace and ease, he did not exercise his authority to correct the evil habits and passions of his children. Rather than contend with them or punish them, he would submit to their will and give them their own way. *Patriarchs and Prophets*, page 575.

We also know that just before Eli died he was overweight. This indicates that Eli was also a man given to appetite. As he could not control his own passions, he could not control the passions of his sons.

We know from the time that Samuel began to minister in the temple that:

> **1 Sam 2:12** Now the sons of Eli were sons of Belial; they knew not the LORD.

We also know that:

> **1 Sam 2:22** Now Eli was very old, and heard all that his sons did unto all Israel; and how they lay with the women that assembled at the door of the tabernacle of the congregation.

Let us keep this in mind as Eli approaches Hannah charging her with being drunk in the temple.

What would be our response to that charge?

1. Knowing that Eli was lax and did not correct his sons.

2. Seeing that this man himself was a slave to appetite.

3. Possibly knowing that Eli's sons were doing very evil things in the temple including marring the sacrifices offered and sleeping with women in the temple.

If we knew these things and were full of pain from the years of taunting from a rival wife, would it not be natural to tell the priest a few home truths? Would it not be reasonable to tell the priest in no uncertain terms that he should deal with the log in his own eye before trying to take the speck out of someone else's eye?

Yet how does Hannah respond?

> **1 Sam 1:15** And Hannah answered and said, No, my lord, I am a woman of a sorrowful spirit: I have drunk neither wine nor strong drink, but have poured out my soul before the LORD.

She sorrowfully responds, "No, my lord."

At the critical moment Hannah maintained the divine pattern and responded in the Spirit of Christ by recognising God's appointed agent.

How do you think Heaven responded to that moment in time? Do you think our Father in Heaven smiled? Do you think He might have shed a tear for joy? This woman had all the reasons in the world to gush forth her pain upon this fat, lax and half blind priest!

Notice the words of blessing that come from the throne of Heaven through this unfit priest.

> **1 Sam 1:17** Then Eli answered and said, Go in peace: and the God of Israel grant thee thy petition that thou hast asked of him.

It was through the blessing of Eli that God gave Hannah peace[2] and it was an act of submission to a corrupt priesthood that brought forth the prophet Samuel.

More than this, Hannah was willing to give her son into the care of this priest who had accused her of being drunk in a previous encounter.

Would you hand your first-born son over to such a man who had spoken to you like that?

What faith! What courage! What an amazing woman!

---

[2] The high priest was deeply moved, for he was a man of God; and in place of rebuke he uttered a blessing: "Go in peace: and the God of Israel grant thee thy petition that thou hast asked of Him." Hannah's prayer was granted; she received the gift for which she had so earnestly entreated. As she looked upon the child, she called him Samuel--"asked of God." *Patriarchs and Prophets*, page 570.

Are there lessons for us today? Are we facing corrupt church leadership, some of whom are meddling with the offerings of the Lord and investing them in dubious places? Are we dealing with men who are lax in restraining younger youth pastors from bringing all kinds of abominations into our church? How do we speak of such ministers when they accuse us of being drunk with wine as we cry in bitterness of soul because of our love for the begotten Son, pleading that this Son should be acknowledged in His church?

Is there a lesson for us? Can blessings come to us through a corrupt channel? Is there a key for us in our situation?

Is it possible that through the very leaders that are doing these things will come the blessing to restore the prophetic voice, a voice that would pronounce judgement on the very structure that was used to produce that voice?

"...He that hath ears to hear, let him hear."

14. Abigail's Sweet Fragrance of Submission

One of the best illustrations of the Spirit of Christ responding to an authority in apostasy is the story of Abigail.

> In the character of Abigail, the wife of Nabal, we have an illustration of womanhood after the order of Christ. *21 Manuscript Release*, page 213.

Nabal has every spiritual advantage as a descendant of Caleb, yet he was everything that a leader should not be. The Bible describes Nabal and Abigail as entirely opposite.

> **1 Sam 25:3** Now the name of the man was Nabal; and the name of his wife Abigail: and s**he was a woman of good understanding, and of a beautiful countenance: but the man was churlish and evil** in his doings; and he was of the house of Caleb.

The word churlish means severe, hard-hearted, obstinate, rough, stubborn, sorrowful and stiff-necked. The word evil here includes adversity, affliction, mischief, naughtiness and wretchedness. The man is a husband from hell. The only good thing mentioned about him was his heritage from Caleb which only heightens the wickedness of his character. Can you imagine what it would have been like for Abigail living with this man? What could be worse than being joined with a severe, rough and wretched husband? Yet in the face of this torrential curse that falls upon Abigail we read in amazement and joy that she was a woman of good understanding and of a beautiful countenance. The Hebrew word good-understanding means:

intelligence; by implication success: - discretion, knowledge, policy, prudence, sense, understanding, wisdom, wise.

How does such a fragrant plant grow in the channel of such a desolate fountain? Is this not the Spirit of Him that became a "root out of a dry (desert/arid) ground?" And so we read:

> The Spirit of the Son of God was abiding in her soul. *Patriarchs and Prophets*, page 667.

The Bible story reveals that David and his men had been providing a hedge of protection for Nabal. David sent a delegation of ten men to Nabal with a blessing and a request. Notice what David told the delegation to tell Nabal:

> **1 Sam 25:6-8** And thus shall ye say to him that liveth in prosperity, **Peace be both to thee, and peace be to thine house, and peace be unto all that thou hast.** (7) And now I have heard that thou hast shearers: now thy shepherds which were with us, we hurt them not, neither was there ought missing unto them, all the while they were in Carmel. (8) Ask thy young men, and they will shew thee. Wherefore let the young men find favour in thine eyes: for we come in a good day: give, I pray thee, whatsoever cometh to thine hand unto thy servants, and to thy son David.

David was the anointed of heaven to bless Israel. The blessing he sent was no mere sweet pleasantry. Those words carried a real blessing for Nabal and his household. The receiving of this blessing only required Nabal to follow the Abrahamic covenant principle of blessing the one who has been blessed of God.

> **Gen 12:2-3** And I will make of thee a great nation, and I will bless thee, and make thy name great; and thou shalt be a blessing: (3) And I will bless them that bless thee, and curse him that curseth thee: and in thee shall all families of the earth be blessed.

There was a blessing for Abigail in the words of David, yet her husband placed himself in a position to bring a curse upon his household and thus a curse upon Abigail.

> **1 Sam 25:10-11** And Nabal answered David's servants, and said, Who is David? and who is the son of Jesse? there

be many servants now a days that break away every man from his master. (11) Shall I then take my bread, and my water, and my flesh that I have killed for my shearers, and give it unto men, whom I know not whence they be?

Notice the challenge that Nabal makes; it sounds very familiar to Pharaoh's response to Moses in Exodus 5:2. Yet Nabal goes beyond Pharaoh's generalised reference and more directly addresses the sonship of David. Nabal refused to acknowledge David's sonship to his father. It was through this line that Jacob had indicated that the sceptre would not depart. Genesis 49:10. The denial of his identity was a direct rejection of his right to rule over Israel.

Mercifully, one of the young men tells Abigail the whole story where it is explained to her that the son of Jesse[1] had been a wall of protection to her husband's flocks and not done anything to harm them. Now the searching question is put to this wise woman:

> **1 Sam 25:17** Now therefore know and consider what thou wilt do; for evil is determined against our master, and against all his household: for he is such a son of Belial, that a man cannot speak to him.

In this statement, the servant is pleading for his own life. He knows that Nabal would not listen to him or any of the servants. Yet if nothing is done, there was a very high risk that David would wipe the entire household off the map.

Abigail makes a decision without her husband's knowledge. She knows that if she pleads with him, she will get the same response she always had received.

> Abigail saw that something must be done to avert the result of Nabal's fault, and that **she must take the responsibility of acting immediately without the counsel of her husband.** She knew that it would be useless to speak to him, for he would only receive her proposition with abuse and contempt. He would remind her that he was the lord of his household, that she was his wife and therefore in subjection to him, and must do as he should dictate. She knew that the evil message must be counteracted immediately, and, without his consent, she gathered together such stores as she thought

---

[1] Jesse means "I possess," and Prov 8:22 says the Lord possessed me in the beginning of His way.

best to conciliate the wrath of David, for she knew he was determined to avenge himself for the insult he had received. She knew also that Nabal was so set and determined in his way that he would never consent to receive her counsel or act upon her plan. She herself brought to David the things that Nabal had refused to give, and bound herself to David's cause for his own good. Abigail's course in this matter was one that God approved, and the circumstance revealed in her a noble spirit and character. *21 Manuscript Release,* page 213.

Let us pause for a moment and consider the life of Abigail living under the tyranny of Nabal. How many times had he mocked her? How many times had he abused her and made her feel like a piece of merchandise? How many times had he denied her those things which a wife should receive from her husband? A man completely stripped of tenderness, thoughtfulness and concern for her welfare. By her approach to David she might have secured her own escape. She could have told David what a wicked man her husband was and then gone on to tell him how badly he was mistreating her. Yet what does inspiration tell us she did?

> Abigail met David with respect, showing him honor and deference, and pleaded her cause eloquently and successfully. While not excusing her husband's insolence, **she still pleaded for his life.** *21 Manuscript Release,* page 214.

I am not sure what emotions are going through your heart right now, but I had to stop and think hard about it. Would you plead for the life of a man that had caused you nothing but misery? Abigail was a beautiful woman inside and out. She understood the channel of blessing. If she cursed her husband then a curse would fall upon her. More than this, she made the following plea to David:

> **1 Sam 25:28** I pray thee, forgive the trespass of thine handmaid: for the LORD will certainly make my lord a sure house; because my lord fighteth the battles of the LORD, and evil hath not been found in thee all thy days.

Abigail asks David to forgive her trespass. WHAT! But Abigail did nothing wrong! Why would she do this? Abigail understood the channel of blessing, and since she was Nabal's wife she owned the sin of her husband in order to confess it. Without truly embracing his sin, she could not truly confess it.

Abigail showed a faith that penetrated deeply into the character of God and His kingdom. In faith she pled for the life of her husband, confessed his sin believing and trusting that God would hear the deeper cry of her heart for freedom from tyranny and freedom to openly honour the son of Jesse.

And so we read:

> **1 Sam 25:36-37** And Abigail came to Nabal; and, behold, he held a feast in his house, like the feast of a king; and Nabal's heart was merry within him, for he was very drunken: wherefore she told him nothing, less or more, until the morning light. (37) But it came to pass in the morning, when the wine was gone out of Nabal, and his wife had told him these things, that his heart died within him, and he became as a stone.

In pleading for the life of her husband, God released her from his tyranny by ending his life.

So we see through a process of pleading for the life of her immediate authority figure and taking his sin upon herself and confessing it, God removed that authority from her and allowed her direct access to David through marriage.

> **1 Cor 10:11** Now all these things happened unto them for ensamples: and they are written for our admonition, upon whom the ends of the world are come.

The Son of God and His angels have been as a wall of protection around the Seventh-day Adventist church. He has sent a delegation to the church with a blessing of peace and a request for a thank offering. Yet our church has lifted up its voice in firm and unrelenting tones[2] and said "Who is the Son of David? We will not have this man reign over us!"

As a consequence, evil is determined for the house of Adventism; messages have come to us to explain the calamity that is about to befall us. Many of us have been treated severely by the church and forbidden to offer thanks to the Son of David in the Adventist household. So what shall we do brothers and sisters? Shall we tell

---

2 "Though some early Adventists struggled with the doctrine, [of the Trinity] our church today has taken a firm and unrelenting stand on this teaching." *Glimpses of our God, Sabbath School Lesson*, Lesson one, Sabbath afternoon, first quarter, 2012.

the Son of David what a wicked man the leadership of Adventism is? Shall we use this as an occasion to free ourselves from its tyranny and plot its destruction through a "providential" circumstance? Shall we not rather release the fragrance of Abigail in our supplications to the Son of David?

> These words could have come only from the lips of one who had partaken of the wisdom from above. The piety of Abigail, like the fragrance of a flower, breathed out all unconsciously in face and word and action. The Spirit of the Son of God was abiding in her soul. Her speech, seasoned with grace, and full of kindness and peace, shed a heavenly influence. *Patriarchs and Prophets*, page 667.

Shall we not plead for the life of our church and for the sins of the church? Shall we not truly own the church's sin in order that we might truly confess it to the Son of David? We don't need the consent of the church to approach the Son of God; we can bring our tributes of praise and plead our case. We certainly don't need the consent of those voices who have already divorced the unfaithful leadership. Let us act quickly and appease the Son of David with our supplications and appeals.

Nabal need not have died. In receiving this news from his wife, he might have discerned her wisdom in saving him, confessed his sin and asked her to forgive him for being so churlish. He might have made amends for his wicked ways, but in maintaining his defiance and refusing to allow the blessing of David to pass though him to Abigail, God removed the blockage in the channel and ensured that Abigail received the gift of peace offered to her in the beginning.

One of the barriers to Nabal changing his ways was his drunken state and his desire to act like a king. If he had been less drunken, he might have changed his ways. Even so, the wine of Babylon that has enticed many in our church is placing many at risk of a heart attack. So we see the most powerful way to remove an obstruction in the channel is to take the sins of that obstruction upon ourselves and plead for the life of those obstructing the channel.

Shall we not plead for their lives? Shall we not pray earnestly for them? Then the words will be pronounced over us:

> **1 Sam 25:32-33** And David said to Abigail, Blessed be the LORD God of Israel, which sent thee this day to meet

me: (33) And blessed be thy advice, and blessed be thou, which hast kept me this day from coming to shed blood, and from avenging myself with mine own hand.

I invite you to read the story of Abigail closely as there are several more instructive points to be gleaned for our benefit. I will mention a few more points for your reflection.

- The story takes place after the death of Samuel, so this story applies to a time period after the death of a prophet. 1 Sam 25:1

- Nabal was a very wealthy man. He was rich and increased with goods and felt he has need of nothing. 1 Sam 25:2

- Even though Saul was ruler and it seemed David might fall victim to Saul's designs, Abigail maintained her faith that the Son of Jesse would rule on the throne of Israel. 1 Sam 25:30

- Abigail was prevented from alerting her husband because of his drunken state. 1 Sam 25:36

- When David called Abigail to be his wife, Abigail took five damsels or virgins with her to the marriage. Does the spirit of Abigail give us a clue to the fragrance of the oil possessed by the wise virgins? 1 Sam 25:42

15. Man After God's Own Heart

The lives of Hannah and Abigail stand as beacons of light for those struggling under the burden of corrupt leadership. The Spirit of Christ in Hannah prepared the way for a mighty prophet to reform the nation of Israel. The fragrant beauty of Abigail steadied the throne of the future monarch through her wise advice given in humble, submissive tones. Both of these women drew down a blessing through a corrupt channel to bless not only themselves but their entire community.

In the life of David we find revealed further vital lessons of how God's people should respond to failed or corrupted leadership. David's case cries out to us with a warning for all those who feel called to do a work for God.

> **1 Sam 16:13** Then Samuel took the horn of oil, and anointed him in the midst of his brethren: and the spirit of the LORD came mightily upon David from that day forward. So Samuel rose up, and went to Ramah.

David was anointed by the highest spiritual authority in Israel to be king of Israel. God had rejected Saul and David was to replace him. What we find most interesting is that David makes no moves to secure for himself that which God had promised him.

> The great honor conferred upon David did not serve to elate him. Notwithstanding the high position which he was to occupy, he quietly continued his employment, content to await the development of the Lord's plans in His own time and way. As humble and modest as before his anointing, the

shepherd boy returned to the hills and watched and guarded his flocks as tenderly as ever. *Patriarchs and Prophets*, page 641.

We see the Lord open the way for David to understand the workings of the king's court by bringing him to play before Saul to refresh the soul of the king. (1 Sam 16:20-23) After David started his rise to prominence within the kingdom, the moody Saul saw him as a dangerous threat.

It is at this point that we see gleams of light in David's character. By now David was married to one of the king's daughters; he knew also that the king's son Jonathan loved him and that many in the community sang his praises. Would not this be the time to assert leadership of the nation? Was he not anointed the future king? Could he not enlist Samuel to his cause, stand in the nation's capital and proclaim himself king? Why all this fleeing from the king when it was in his power to turn the people to his cause? Let's summarise David's situation:

1. He was ordained by the highest spiritual authority and former judge of Israel to be king.

2. He was a national hero after slaying Goliath.

3. He was married to a king's daughter.

4. He was loved by the next in line to the throne, Jonathan.

5. David was a skilled general that now led a band of lethal fighters, fresh from destroying scores of Philistines.

Why run from Saul? He had slain Goliath single-handedly. Would not God deliver Saul into his hand to take the throne? So what do we find happening in Scripture?

> **1 Sam 24:2-4** Then Saul took three thousand chosen men out of all Israel, and went to seek David and his men upon the rocks of the wild goats. (3) And he came to the sheepcotes by the way, where was a cave; and Saul went in to cover his feet: and David and his men remained in the sides of the cave. (4) And the men of David said unto him, Behold the day of which the LORD said unto thee, Behold, I will deliver thine enemy into thine hand, that thou mayest

> do to him as it shall seem good unto thee. Then David arose, and cut off the skirt of Saul's robe privily.

If you were in that cave, and peering through the darkness to see the same man who wanted you dead lying fast asleep after coming into the very cave in which you are hiding, surely, you would have to see this as divine providence. Surely, you would reason that since you are the Lord's anointed and future monarch, you must stop the suffering of Israel and walk through the door that God had obviously provided for you, shouldn't you?

> **1 Sam 24:6-7** And he said unto his men, The LORD forbid that I should do this thing unto my master, the LORD'S anointed, to stretch forth mine hand against him, seeing he is the anointed of the LORD. (7) So David stayed his servants with these words, and suffered them not to rise against Saul. But Saul rose up out of the cave, and went on his way.

WHAT! This demon possessed madman who is wasting precious resources trying to kill the very man who God has called to be king! What does David call this man? "The Lord's anointed!"

As one of David's men, wouldn't you try and reason with him? Maybe he is young and inexperienced? Maybe he is not discerning the will of God and needs a little Judas style assistance to cause him to seize the throne that providence so obviously is providing!

This story is not only astounding for the fact that David said what he said, but that the men who were with him did not answer him a word but accepted his counsel.

Oh Father in heaven, how we need men filled with this Spirit now. Please send us this Spirit to help us see the right way to deal with failed leadership. I ask this in the name of your Son, Jesus.

Just in case we missed this point, David takes us through the whole routine again for good measure in 1 Samuel 26. I invite you to read the chapter carefully but here is the principle expressed again.

> **1 Sam 26:9-11** And David said to Abishai, Destroy him not: for who can stretch forth his hand against the LORD'S anointed, and be guiltless? (10) David said furthermore, As the LORD liveth, the LORD shall smite him; or his day shall come to die; or he shall descend into battle, and

perish. (11) The LORD forbid that I should stretch forth mine hand against the LORD'S anointed: but, I pray thee, take thou now the spear that is at his bolster, and the cruse of water, and let us go.

These words ring in my ears like the rolling thunder from Sinai.

...who can put forth his hand against the LORD'S anointed, and be guiltless?

My friends, are not these stories written for our admonition? Can we not discern in this a lesson for how we should respond to failed leadership? If a man such as David acted like this towards such a poor, deceived, weak, moody, possessed man as Saul, what is our excuse?

Lest we miss some of the deeper significance of 1 Samuel 24 and 26, notice the blessings that came forth from Saul to David.

1 Sam 24:17-20 And he said to David, Thou art more righteous than I: for thou hast rendered unto me good, whereas I have rendered unto thee evil. (18) And thou hast declared this day how that thou hast dealt well with me: forasmuch as when the LORD had delivered me up into thine hand, thou killedst me not. (19) For if a man find his enemy, will he let him go well away? wherefore the LORD reward thee good for that thou hast done unto me this day. (20) And now, behold, I know that thou shalt surely be king, and that the kingdom of Israel shall be established in thine hand.

From the word of the apostate king came the declaration of kingship for David; from the mouth of the perverse came a blessing for David and Israel. Like Baalim, Saul desired to curse Israel by destroying David, but in the hands of the Almighty, he could do nothing but bless him! Hallelujah, Praise to our Father.

Luke 18:27 And he said, The things which are impossible with men are possible with God

But our Father does not draw just once from this perverted well, He stoops down again to show us that He is not mocked and that His Sovereign Will cannot be overturned by any man.

1 Sam 26:25 Then Saul said to David, Blessed be thou, my son David: thou shalt both do great things, and also shalt

still prevail. So David went on his way, and Saul returned to his place.

All these things that Saul pronounced over David took place. David prevailed and did great things and was made king of Israel according to the word of the king.

How thankful I am for these Biblical examples of dealing with failed leadership. The sons of Belial will cry out with all manner of reasons for why this does not apply to us, but I am convinced that these stories are written specifically for us at this time. Let us not lay our hands or our mouths upon the Lord's anointed, but rather, let us wait for God to establish the path of the just.

Section 5. Sanctified Through the Divine Pattern

16. Unmasking the Abominable Desolator

The purpose of this book is to try and draw down some practical implications of what our understanding of the Father and Son relationship does to our families, churches and communities in terms of blessing or cursing. I am trying to show that there is a world of difference between the "Son" in the Trinity and the Son of the living God as revealed in Scripture. Hopefully by now you will have the picture that every aspect of our life experience is touched and affected in some way.

In this chapter I want to explore the transaction that is described in Daniel 7 and 8. This transaction of the coming of the Son of Man to the Ancient of Days is the central pillar and foundation of Adventism. This is the source of our power for knowing what it means to enter the Most Holy Place. How we understand the central characters in this transaction will therefore filter down into every other doctrine we hold; that is, of course, if it is our central pillar.

> The Scripture which above all others had been both the foundation and the central pillar of the advent faith was the declaration: "Unto two thousand and three hundred days; then shall the sanctuary be cleansed." Daniel 8:14. *Great Controversy*, page 409.

The more real we understand this narrative the more real becomes the whole Investigative Judgement experience. I want to suggest to you that only the divine pattern as revealed in 1 Corinthians 8:6 can give real meaning to the transaction between the Ancient of Days and the Son of Man.

Let us consider parts of this narrative carefully.

> **Dan 7:9,10,13,14** I beheld till the thrones were cast down, and the Ancient of days did sit, whose garment was white as snow, and the hair of his head like the pure wool: his throne was like the fiery flame, and his wheels as burning fire. (10) A fiery stream issued and came forth from before him: thousand thousands ministered unto him, and ten thousand times ten thousand stood before him: the judgment was set, and the books were opened. ... (13) **I saw in the night visions, and, behold, one like the Son of man came with the clouds of heaven, and came to the Ancient of days, and they brought him near before him. (14) And there was given him dominion, and glory, and a kingdom**, that all people, nations, and languages, should serve him: his dominion is an everlasting dominion, which shall not pass away, and his kingdom that which shall not be destroyed.

What is our perception of reality in this story? Is there a real person who is the Ancient of Days? Does He sit? Are His garments as white as snow? Is the hair of His head white like pure wool? Were there actual books opened? Was the Son of Man actually brought in before Him?

I have another question I want to ask you, but before I ask that I want to show you a difference in understanding between our pioneers and current scholarship.

I want you to read how Uriah Smith understood this. This is from *Bible Student's Assistant,* pages 45-46 - Uriah Smith 1858.[1]

GOD A PERSONAL BEING

PROOF. "The Father himself which hath sent me, hath borne witness of me. Ye have neither heard his VOICE at any time, nor seen HIS SHAPE." John 5:37.

"God who . . . spake in time past unto the fathers by the prophets, hath in these last days spoken unto us by his Son, . . . who being the brightness of his glory and the express IMAGE of his PERSON," etc. Heb.1:1-4.

---

[1] Capitalisation in original

"I beheld till the. . . . Ancient of Days did sit, whose garment was white as snow, and the HAIR of his HEAD like the pure wool." Dan.7:9.

"And (Moses) said, I beseech Thee, shew me thy glory. . . . And he said, Thou canst not see my FACE; for there shall no man see me and live. And the Lord said, Behold there is a place by me, and thou shalt stand upon a rock: and it shall come to pass while my glory passeth by, that I will put thee in a cleft of the rock, and will cover thee with my HAND while I pass by. And I will take away mine hand, and thou shalt see my BACK PARTS, but my FACE shall not be seen." Ex.33:18-23. [46] "And they heard the voice of the Lord WALKING in the garden in the cool of the day." Gen.3:8. "And they saw the God of Israel, and there was under his FEET as it were a paved work of sapphire stone." Ex.24:10.

"After the Lord had spoken unto them, he was received up into heaven, and SAT on the RIGHT HAND OF GOD." Mark 16:19. "Hast thou an ARM =like God? or canst thou thunder with a VOICE like HIM?" Job 40:9. "Out of the mouth of the Most High proceedeth not evil and good." Lam.3:38.

Now listen to James White:

James White – *Review and Herald,* August 19, 1858.

What is God? He is a material, organized intelligence, possessing both body and parts. He is in the form of man. What is Jesus Christ? He is the Son of God, and is like his Father, being "the brightness of his Father's glory, and the express image of his person." He is a material intelligence, with body, parts and passions; possessing immortal flesh and immortal bones.

Now contrast the previous statements with the following:

Bible Questions Answered By DON F. NEUFELD - *Review and Herald*, October 6, 1977.

Worthy of note is the fact that this statement makes no comment on whether the members of the Godhead have physical or material bodies. Adventists have been reticent to speculate as to this aspect of God's nature. Speaking of Him, they emphasize His attributes, such as personality, self-existence, transcendence, immutability, omniscience, omnipresence, omnipotence, holiness, and love. **It's true that in the Bible, God is represented as having ears (Ps. 17:6), nostrils (2 Sam.22:9), a mouth (Deut. 8:3), a hand (Zech. 2:9), feet (Ps.18:9). But these are usually considered as being anthropomorphisms, that is, expressions attributing to God human characteristics. They are attempts; it is claimed, to help human beings understand God, who is much above them?**

Do you see the difference? Let us go back to the pioneers and let them explain their position a little more. Let James White set the context for us.

Our position is, that a change has taken place in the position and work of our literal High Priest in the literal Sanctuary in heaven, which is to be compared to the coming of the bridegroom in the marriage. **This view is a perfect safeguard against spiritualism.[2] We not only believe in a literal Jesus, who is a "Minister of the Sanctuary," but we also believe that the Sanctuary is literal**. - And more, when John says that he saw "one like the Son of man" "in the midst of the seven candlesticks," that is, in the Holy Place, we know not how to make the candlestick spiritual, and the Son of man literal. We therefore believe that both are literal, and that John saw Jesus while a "Minister" in the Holy Place. John also had a view of another part of the Sanctuary, which view applies to the time of the sounding of the seventh angel.

...The Most Holy, containing the Ark of the ten commandments, was then opened for our Great High Priest to enter to make atonement for the cleansing of the Sanctuary. **If we take the liberty to say there is not a literal Ark, containing the ten commandments in heaven, we may go only a step further and deny the literal City, and the literal Son of God. Certainly, Adventists should**

---

[2] Spiritualism meaning a method of Bible study

not choose the spiritual view, rather than the one we have presented. We see no middle ground to be taken. *The Parable*, page 16.

James White understood the issues at stake. He knew that if the scenes of the Judgement from Daniel 7 and 8 were not literally taking place then the whole doctrine would collapse in on itself. Notice how Joseph Bates answers the next question I wish to ask and that is:

Does the Ancient of Days actually give a dominion and kingdom to the Son of Man?

> And Daniel, the prophet, teaches the same doctrine. "I saw in the night visions: and behold, one like the Son of man came with the clouds of heaven, and came to the Ancient of days, (described in the ninth verse) and they brought him near before him; and there was given him dominion and glory, and a kingdom, never to be destroyed." Dan. 7:13,14. Now we all admit this personage was Jesus Christ; for no being on earth or in heaven, has ever had the promise of an everlasting kingdom but him. **And does not the Ancient of days give it to him? Would it not be absurd to say that he gave it to himself? How then can it be said (or proved) as it is by some, that the Son is the Ancient of days; - this passage, and the one in fifth Revelations, distinctly prove God and his Son to be two persons in heaven. Jesus says, "I proceeded forth and came from God: neither came I of myself, but he sent me." John 8:42. "I come forth from the Father, and am come into the world; again, I leave the world and go to the Father**." Joseph Bates, 1846, *Opening of the Heavens*, page 18.

Can you see how the pioneers answered this question? Can you see how their rejection of the Trinity caused them to see that the Ancient of Days was exactly what that title means—Ancient of Days? He therefore had absolute authority to grant a kingdom to His Son.

Please do not miss this point as it reveals the secret of Seventh-day Adventism's long flowing hair and is the secret of her power. The reality of the Heavenly Sanctuary, the reality of the mediatorial work of Jesus, the reality of His receiving a kingdom all depend on a clear understanding of the distinct personalities of Father and Son. Any shift towards a metaphorical understanding because of a Trinitarian mindset and this whole system collapses. It appears as a mirage on the dusty walls of scholars' minds serving only as an illustration but is not real.

It is impossible for a Trinitarian mind to actually believe that the Father is giving a literal kingdom to His Son. It can only be a symbolic gesture for the purposes of the plan of salvation, and this is the desolating genius of the Trinity. It forces the mind into a metaphorical gear and then strips the mind of the realism of the Sanctuary, the Son of Man and the Ancient of Days. These realities are replaced with metaphorical labels that are just hung on a wall for us to admire as if we were in an art gallery.

When we believe that Jesus is the "By Whom" agent of the Father, then the whole Sanctuary narrative springs to life and finds traction in the soul as being a real event. This is why our pioneers spoke so often about the distinct personalities of Father and Son. Notice:

> Those who seek to remove the old landmarks are not holding fast; they are not remembering how they have received and heard. Those who try to bring in theories that would remove **the pillars of our faith concerning the sanctuary or concerning the personality of God or of Christ**, are working as blind men. They are seeking to bring in uncertainties and to set the people of God adrift without an anchor. *Manuscript Releases* 760, page 9.

> We are now to be on guard, and not drawn away from the all-important message given of God for this time. **Satan is not ignorant of the result of trying to define God and Jesus Christ in a spiritualistic[3] way that sets God and Christ as a nonentity**. The moments occupied in this kind of science are, in the place of preparing the way of the Lord, making a way for Satan to come in and confuse the minds with mysticisms of his own devising. Although they are dressed up in angel robes they have made our God and our Christ a nonentity. Why?--because Satan sees the minds are all fitted for his working. Men have lost tract of Christ and

---

[3] [USED HERE IN REFERENCE TO A SYSTEM OF INTERPRETATION, NOT SPIRITISM POPULARLY CALLED SPIRITUALISM.] This comment in caps was inserted here by White Estate.

the Lord God, and have been obtaining an experience that is Omega to one of the most subtle delusions that will ever captivate the minds of men. We are forbidden to . . . set the imagination in a train of conjecture. *11 Manuscript Releases*, page 211.

Can you see why Ellen White connects the doctrine of the Sanctuary to the personalities of the Father and the Son? As you read the Fundamental statement of Adventists on the Trinity do you see a clear distinction of Father and Son?

2. Trinity:

There is one God: Father, Son, and Holy Spirit, a unity of three co-eternal Persons. God is immortal, all-powerful, all-knowing, above all, and ever present. **He** is infinite and beyond human comprehension, yet known through **His** self-revelation. **He** is forever worthy of worship, adoration, and service by the whole creation. (Deut. 6:4; Matt. 28:19; 2 Cor. 13:14; Eph. 4:4-6; 1 Peter 1:2; 1 Tim. 1:17; Rev. 14:7.)

In this statement the One God is three persons, which are then referenced as "He" and "His." When you read the "He" and the "His," who are you thinking about? I find this statement confusing. "He" in English refers to a singular being.

See how some of our Adventist Scholars describe this god:

We would suggest that God in **His Trinitarian self-revelation**, has claimed that **He** created us to reflect the love that supernaturally resides in **His** very being as an eternally loving **God who is one in three**. Furthermore, **the triune love found in God** is not self-oriented and thus strongly implies that we find our greatest joy and satisfaction in living and serving others. Whidden, Moon and Reeve, *The Trinity*, page 247.

See how the language used is "He" and "His" and then combined with the term "Trinitarian self-revelation." Notice again how the word "He" also means "They" in the following statement:

"In the doctrine of the Trinity, we do not find three different divine roles displayed by one Person (that is modalism). Nor are there three gods in a cluster (that

113

is tritheism or polytheism). **The one God ("He") is also, and equally, "They," and "They" are always together**, always closely cooperating. The Holy Spirit executes the will of both Father and Son, which is also His will. This is the truth that God reveals about Himself all through the Bible. *Glimpses of Our God, Adult Sabbath School Bible Study Guide*, Lesson 1, 1st Quarter 2012, Principal Contributor: Jo Ann Davidson.

Does this not make indistinct the personalities of Father and Son? Please note this frank admission from an Adventist theologian about the difficulty in maintaining a clear distinction of persons in the Trinity:

> The difficulty is evident enough. **A doctrine that affirms that God is one, and yet that there are three persons in God, must often bewilder the mind in its attempt to find a relevant and intelligible framework in which that seeming contradiction can be expressed and at the same time meet the average person's religious needs**. No wonder that the reference to the Father incomprehensible, the Son incomprehensible, and the Holy Spirit incomprehensible has encouraged sardonic remarks to the effect that the whole doctrine is incomprehensible. Raoul Dederen. '*Reflections on the Doctrine of the Trinity*,' 1970. Andrews University.

Here is the secret of Satan's Desolation of the Heavenly Sanctuary. It comes through a merging of the Son with the Father caused by a Trinitarian formula of three persons in one god. As soon as you have that formula in place, the narrative of Daniel 7 and 8 is desolated.

Only the "Of Whom" and "By Whom" understanding of Father and Son allow us to keep them distinct in our minds and give real meaning to the Daniel 7 story.

17. The Cornerstone

In this book we have been beholding the divine pattern of Father and Son as reflected in many aspects of our families, communities and churches. By simply beholding this divine pattern in faith through Christ we will be transformed into their likeness as the Bible states:

> **2 Cor 3:18** But we all, with open face beholding as in a glass the glory of the Lord, are changed into the same image from glory to glory, even as by the Spirit of the Lord.

While some members of society are given positions to copy aspects of the "Of Whom" role of the Father, all of us are to look to the Son of God as the chief "By Whom" pattern that all of us must copy to receive the blessing and life of the Father. The Son of God is therefore the chief Cornerstone, the first born of all creation that we might pattern after Him. This is why the government was placed upon His shoulders in order that Christ might be the everlasting Father of all those who submit to the one true God – the Ancient of Days.

This is why:

> **Phil 2:9-11** Wherefore God also hath highly exalted him, and given him a name which is above every name: (10) That at the name of Jesus every knee should bow, of things in heaven, and things in earth, and things under the earth; (11) And that every tongue should confess that Jesus Christ is Lord, to the glory of God the Father.

Since Jesus is the Cornerstone of all creation, it is Satan's studied effort to alter our perceptions of this Cornerstone; to cause us to pattern after a cheap worthless imitation that appears similar to the original Stone in many aspects, but is really completely different.

In the first chapter we noted:

> The rebellion of Satan introduced concepts and ideas that marred this divine pattern. The order of Heaven meant that originally Lucifer was under the authority of Christ, who was under the authority of His Father... The Scripture tells us how Satan wished to alter the divine pattern:
>
> **Isa 14:12-14** How art thou fallen from heaven, O Lucifer, son of the morning! how art thou cut down to the ground, which didst weaken the nations! (13) For thou hast said in thine heart, I will ascend into heaven, I will exalt my throne above the stars of God: I will sit also upon the mount of the congregation, in the sides of the north: (14) I will ascend above the heights of the clouds; I will be like the most High.
>
> In these texts we see a being who does not seek to be under the protection and care of the divine pattern but rather seeks to be like, meaning to resemble, the Most High ... Through a cunning process Satan has deceived the Christian world into making Christ exactly the same as the Father. As the Christian world worships God through its various creeds, the entity perceived as the second person of the Godhead is actually a formulation of Satan. By presenting Christ as exactly the same as the Father in every way, Satan confuses the human mind through the law of indiscernibility; meaning that two things possess the exact same qualities so that they no longer can be clearly discerned separately, they become mysteriously one through their loss of individuality.

Satan has altered the Cornerstone of Christianity from a Son who inherited all things from His Father as a separate and distinct being, to a being that possessed all things from himself or by virtue of the fact that he is part of a three-person-yet-one being God. The difference between these two can be summed up, as a being that comes in his own name rather than coming in the name of His Father.

The Divine Pattern

> **John 5:43** I am come in my Father's name, and ye receive me not: if another shall come in his own name, him ye will receive.

The Biblical Cornerstone looks to the absolute authority of His Father for direction, counsel and blessing. He does not rely on the inherited powers He possesses to guide Him but rather on the one who bestowed the inheritance. He uses His powers as directed by His Father. The counterfeit cornerstone stands shoulder to shoulder with the other divine persons resting in his own divine qualities and offering counsel, guidance and advice as much as he receives it. He works in a democratic manner of co-equal collaboration.

The Biblical Cornerstone finds equality by the Word of His Father and that alone. He does not think it robbery to be equal with God because God commanded that He was to be equal with the Father. The counterfeit cornerstone finds equality in his age, his omnipotence, his power, his knowledge and his might. He needs no word from the other divine persons for he is already equal based upon his own resources.

After which cornerstone have many of us been patterning all our lives? Do wives find equality with their husbands through the Word of the Father, patterning themselves after Christ and like Him willingly serve in their appointed positions? Men, do you faithfully serve in your community and church knowing you are equal to other men as brethren, yet serve in the appointed "By Whom" channel patterning yourself after Christ?

What cornerstone are you building upon? What is your house resting upon?

> **1 Pet 2:6-7** Wherefore also it is contained in the scripture, Behold, I lay in Sion a chief corner stone, elect, precious: and he that believeth on him shall not be confounded. (7) Unto you therefore which believe he is precious: but unto them which be disobedient, the stone which the builders disallowed, the same is made the head of the corner,

Our Father has laid a chief Cornerstone and it is from this Stone that we are to pattern ourselves. As the Scripture states:

> **1 Cor 3:11** For other foundation can no man lay than that is laid, which is Jesus Christ.

The Cornerstone

The Bible has declared emphatically that Jesus is none other than the divine Son of God by inheritance.

> **Matt 16:15-18** He saith unto them, But whom say ye that I am? (16) And Simon Peter answered and said, Thou art the Christ, the Son of the living God. (17) And Jesus answered and said unto him, Blessed art thou, Simon Barjona: for flesh and blood hath not revealed it unto thee, but my Father which is in heaven. (18) And I say also unto thee, That thou art Peter, and upon this rock I will build my church; and the gates of hell shall not prevail against it.

> **Heb 1:3-4** Who being the brightness of his glory, and the express image of his person, and upholding all things by the word of his power, when he had by himself purged our sins, sat down on the right hand of the Majesty on high; (4) Being made so much better than the angels, as he hath by inheritance obtained a more excellent name than they.

> **John 8:42** Jesus said unto them, If God were your Father, ye would love me: for I proceeded forth[1] and came from God; neither came I of myself, but he sent me.

Notice how Jesus refers to the disciples who followed Him; see what cornerstone they had chosen.

> **John 17:8** For I have given unto them the words which thou gavest me; and they have received them, and have known surely that I came out[2] from thee, and they have believed that thou didst send me.

Yet this Cornerstone is a rock of offense to many. They do not wish to build their house on a rock that looks to another being as an absolute authority over them. They would rather build upon a being that is equal by his power, his talent, his gifts and abilities. Notice the words of one Adventist scholar on this very point:

---

[1] Strongs: exerchomai From G1537 and G2064; to issue (literally or figuratively): - come-(forth, out), depart (out of), escape, get out, go (abroad, away, forth, out, thence), proceed (forth), spread abroad.

[2] exerchomai. Same word as that used in John 8:42 - "proceeded forth." The use of the word cannot simply mean "to leave the presence of" as this is addressed in the rest of the verse "and they have believed that thou didst send me." Exerchomai always means "to come out of." This reveals Christ's reference to being begotten or brought forth from the Father.

> Shortly we shall see that the monarchical conception of the Trinity is reflected especially in the hierarchical structure of the Catholic Church, where the pope acts as God's official representative on earth, invested with special powers to govern the church. The outcome of this monarchical practice is the passive submission of believers who fail to exercise their spiritual gifts within the body of Christ. By contrast, the biblical view of the Trinity as perfect communion of the Three, gives rise to a community of believers with a variety of gifts that are valued and exercised as expressing the communion of the Trinity itself. Samuel Bacchiocchi – *Endtime Issues Newsletter No. 147* – "The Importance of the Doctrine of the Trinity."

Did you see how the writer presented the notion of a hierarchical structure as Catholic and the idea of a being who is invested with power as simply Papal? This is then contrasted with his understanding of God who are/is a perfect communion of three and which value each other because of their variety of gifts. The correct Cornerstone concept of invested power is merged with the Papal system as a means of casting aside the Cornerstone in favour of the counterfeit which finds value in the variety of gifts possessed by the individual members.

This is the new cornerstone of Adventism. As the church seeks to pattern itself on this new perfect communion of three with a flattened relational structure, we see members forsaking the principle of submission and seeking to share their gifts in the church in order to be valued and appreciated.

If you are a simple labouring man and only hold a deacon's position in the church, then you will be appreciated far less than the man who is an elder who preaches and does Bible studies. And this man will be less valued than the man who has an international ministry preaching the gospel to the entire world. Of course, we can't say those things openly! "We only engage these roles for the love of the truth," and therefore all our board meetings are sweet and filled with the spirit of submission and grace, and there are never any power struggles – are there?

The new cornerstone of Adventism causes people to pattern themselves in a way to have an urgent need to be in some kind of ministry. The world needs to be blessed by their gifts because this is how the counterfeit Jesus is valued by the "Father" and "Spirit" – because of his variety of gifts.

The Biblical Cornerstone is a rock of offense to the spirit of this world. The Biblical Cornerstone does not find value in His variety of gifts but only in the Word of His Father. Therefore Jesus is:

> **1 Pet 2:8** … a stone of stumbling, and a rock of offence, even to them which stumble at the word, being disobedient: whereunto also they were appointed.

We as a people were appointed to believe on Jesus as the Son of God, but our church has stumbled at the Word and become disobedient. Jesus stated:

> **Luke 20:17-18** And he beheld them, and said, What is this then that is written, The stone which the builders rejected, the same is become the head of the corner? (18) Whosoever shall fall upon that stone shall be broken; but on whomsoever it shall fall, it will grind him to powder.

Those who look to the begotten Son and fall upon this rock are having their hard hearts broken up and softened, changed and moulded into the image of the divine Son. Those who refuse this Cornerstone will have that stone fall upon them and crush them to powder.

So we have before us the true cornerstone who comes in His Father's name and is fully under His Father's authority and we have another who calls himself the "Son of the Father" (Barabbas)[3] and yet comes in His own name as a thief and a robber.[4] Whom shall you choose, Christ or Barabbas?

Let us build on the Cornerstone that inherited all things from His Father and learn like Jesus to rest in the Father's blessed authority, protection and provision.

---

[3] Barabbas = "son of a father or master" - Thayer

[4] "Barabbas had pretended to be Christ and had done great wickedness. . . . A most striking contrast was presented between the two. Barabbas was a notorious character who had done wonderful things through satanic agencies. He claimed to have religious power, a right to establish a different order of things. This false Christ was claiming what Satan claimed in heaven—a right to all things. Christ in His humiliation was possessor of all things. In Him was no darkness at all. . . ." *Manuscript* 112, 1897

18. Sabbath Sealing

As God's people we know that it is the faithful observance of the Sabbath that reveals God's ownership of a person. We also know that it is through the sanctifying power of the Sabbath that God's people will be sealed.

> **Ezek 20:12** Moreover also I gave them my sabbaths, to be a sign between me and them, that they might know that I am the LORD that sanctify them.

In chapter 2 we explored the fountain structure of the law that reflects the divine pattern at the centre. It is through this divine pattern that the Spirit of God flows to us, sanctifies us and gives us overcoming power. There is nothing more wonderful than a community based on family values worshipping together on Sabbath. This fully opens the fountain in the law to us. Notice what Ellen White says:

> True sanctification is harmony with God, oneness with Him in character. It is received through obedience to those principles that are the transcript of His character. **And the Sabbath is the sign of obedience. He who from the heart obeys the fourth commandment will obey the whole law. He is sanctified through obedience**... To us as to Israel the Sabbath is given "for a perpetual covenant." To those who reverence His holy day the Sabbath is a sign that God recognizes them as His chosen people. *Testimonies, Volume 6*, page 350.

Sabbath Sealing

The Sabbath brings to God's people a sweet outpouring of the Spirit of God. The more we desire this Sabbath blessing and make preparation for it, the more of the Living Bread we will have to eat.[1]

Since there is a wonderful blessing in the Sabbath, we know that Satan will be on the ground contesting every inch to stop us from receiving this blessing.

This is where the divine pattern becomes important. The Sabbath principle is one of rest from our labours. Only those who are able to rest in the channel of blessing can truly rest from their labours.

In the previous chapter we examined the true Cornerstone and Its counterfeit. I wanted to present these thoughts as a basis for understanding the Sabbath sealing more clearly.

Someone who is patterning themselves after a cornerstone that finds value in sharing their gifts in their family, community and church, will find it very hard to prepare for the Sabbath and indeed rest on the Sabbath. The counterfeit cornerstone is going to create pressure on Friday afternoon. The desire to work on things that reveal our talent and ability comes up against the need to cease from labour. This is not just a ceasing from physical labour, but from all mental activity that relates to our work. There are many who cease their physical labour on Friday afternoon and yet during Sabbath hours are planning, thinking and pondering what they will do after Sabbath.

If we are building on the true Cornerstone, then the need to perform and achieve begins to reduce; Sabbath preparation becomes easier and the Sabbath becomes sweeter.

I can testify that before I began to pattern after the true Cornerstone, Friday afternoon was always a rush. We often would be doing final minute jobs as the sun was setting. For a time we decided not to get "legalistic" about things, and we sadly violated the edges of the Sabbath.

As I turned to the true Cornerstone, I became more and more convicted about the Sabbath. I was under deep conviction that we should be able to be in a completely meditative state of mind at least half an hour before the sun went down and have all showering and

---

[1] I cover this in detail in my presentation, "The Law of the Wise," if you want to explore this in greater depth. http://vimeo.com/15831639.

preparations finished well before sunset. I was convicted this must be done in a spirit of peace and happiness rather than rushed frustration. Rarely in all my Adventist life had I been able to welcome the Sabbath with both heart and mind fully resting and eagerly waiting for the Sabbath to arrive.

I am able to report with joy that this has now changed. The habits of decades took time to change. At first we had to reserve all of Friday just for house cleaning and preparation. Even then we found we would sometimes only just make it. Our spirits were still troubled due to the stress we felt in getting ready. But the more we have beheld the divine pattern the easier Sabbath preparation has become.

What a delight the Sabbath has become. What a joy to be seated well before the setting of the sun and to be meditating on the Word of God and praising Him before the sun sets.

> What is the condition of those who keep the commandments of God and have the faith of Jesus? If in families there are those who are refusing [plus ignoring/failing] obedience to the Lord in keeping His Sabbath, then the seal cannot be placed upon them. The sealing is a pledge from God of perfect security to His chosen ones (Exodus 31:13-17). Sealing indicates you are God's chosen. He has appropriated you to Himself. As the sealed of God we are Christ's purchased possession, and no one shall pluck us out of His hands. The seal given in the forehead is God, New Jerusalem. "I will write upon him the name of My God, and the name of the city of My God" (Revelation 3:12). *15 Manuscript Releases*, page 225.

For those who have studied this subject carefully we know that God's seal is found in the Sabbath. His Name, Title and Dominion are only found in this commandment. It is also interesting to note that:

> **Rev 14:1** And I looked, and, lo, a Lamb stood on the mount Sion, and with him an hundred forty and four thousand, having his Father's name written in their foreheads.

The Spirit of Prophecy states:

> **John saw a Lamb on Mount Zion, and with him 144,000, having his Father's name written in their foreheads. They bore the signet of heaven.** They reflected the image of God. They were full of the light and the glory of the Holy

One. If we would have the image and superscription of God upon us, we must separate ourselves from all iniquity. We must forsake every evil way, and then we must trust our cases in the hands of Christ. While we are working out our own salvation with fear and trembling, God will work in us to will and to do of his own good pleasure. While you must do your part, yet it is God that must give you aid, and sanctify you. Christ makes us penitent that he may forgive us. We have an idea that we must do some part of the work alone. We have thought that there are two or three steps that we must take without any help or support. But this is not so. The Spirit of God is continually wooing and drawing the soul to right purposes, and into harmony with the law of God. The invitation is given to the helpless, "Ho, every one that thirsteth, come ye to the waters, and he that hath no money; come ye, buy, and eat; yea, come, buy wine and milk, without money and without price." As soon as we separate ourselves from evil, and choose to serve God, we shall respond to this invitation. *Review and Herald*, March 19, 1889.

The writing of the Father's name in the forehead is a writing of exactly what that name means – Father. Our recognition of God as the Father of our Lord Jesus Christ establishes the divine pattern of the "Of Whom" and "By Whom." Seeing the Father as the great source of all[2] causes us to see the Son as one who inherits all and rests in the Father's Word. When we see Christ in this Cornerstone capacity we are enabled to be changed into His image and therefore learn to rest upon the Sabbath. By this process we are sealed and prepared for the final crisis.

I have found in both the Word of God and my personal experience, that the counterfeit cornerstone caused me to lightly regard the Sabbath[3] and to push my projects right to the edges of the Sabbath

---

[2] "'I seek not Mine own glory, but the glory of Him that sent Me.' John 8:28; 6:57; 8:50; 7:18. In these words is set forth the great principle which is the law of life for the universe. All things Christ received from God, but He took to give. So in the heavenly courts, in His ministry for all created beings: through the beloved Son, the Father's life flows out to all; through the Son it returns, in praise and joyous service, a tide of love, to the great Source of all. And thus through Christ the circuit of beneficence is complete, representing the character of the great Giver, the law of life." *Desire of Ages*, page 21.

[3] "The Sabbath of course, would be lightly regarded, as also the God who created it." 1 *Selected Messages*, page 205.

and indeed often into the Sabbath hours. Through the false Christ presented to me in the Trinity I was prevented from receiving the sealing experience of the Sabbath.

Those who do not accept Jesus as the Son of the Father do not in fact believe that God is the Father of our Lord Jesus Christ. Yet it is this name – "The Father" – that will be sealed into the foreheads of faithful children.

Modern translations alter this verse and indicate that it is the Father's name and the Lamb's name:

> **Rev 14:1** ASV And I saw, and behold, the Lamb standing on the mount Zion, and with him a hundred and forty and four thousand, having his name, and the name of his Father, written on their foreheads.

Yet we know that the Lamb has His Father' name.

> **Exo 23:20-21** Behold, I send an Angel before thee, to keep thee in the way, and to bring thee into the place which I have prepared. (21) Beware of him, and obey his voice, provoke him not; for he will not pardon your transgressions: for my name is in him.

Since the Lamb has the Father's name in Him, as we pattern ourselves on Him, we become like Him and also have the Father's name as Christ does. As Jesus told us:

> **John 20:17** …I ascend unto my Father, and your Father; and to my God and your God.

Brethren, I appeal to you to set your houses in order in a calm, peaceful and joyful manner to be ready for the Sabbath, if this is not happening already. Nothing must stand in the way of being ready before the sun sets and to have our hearts filled with praise and thanksgiving to God and the Lamb. This preparation becomes easier and easier as we behold the divine pattern and learn to rest in the Father's love, even as our Lord Jesus rests in His Father's Word.

19. A Mighty Angel

Rev 18:1-2 And after these things I saw another angel come down from heaven, having great power;[1] and the earth was lightened with his glory. (2) And he cried mightily with a strong voice, saying, Babylon the great is fallen, is fallen, and is become the habitation of devils, and the hold of every foul spirit, and a cage of every unclean and hateful bird.

What I have tried to present in this book is simply this:[2]

This message was to bring more prominently before the world the uplifted Saviour, the sacrifice for the sins of the whole world. It presented justification through faith in the Surety; it invited the people to receive the righteousness of Christ, which is made manifest in obedience to all the commandments of God. **Many had lost sight of Jesus** [because of a counterfeit cornerstone]. They needed to have their eyes directed to His divine person [as distinct from the Father], His merits [the divine "By Whom," sacrifice and true mediator to the Father], and His changeless love for the human family. **All power is given** [by the Father – "Of Whom"] **into His hands, that He may dispense** ["By Whom"] rich gifts unto men, imparting the priceless gift of His own righteousness to the helpless human agent. This is the message that God commanded to be given to the world. It is the third angel's message, which is to be proclaimed with

---

[1] Strongs: ...authority, jurisdiction, liberty, power, right, strength.

[2] Comments in square brackets supplied.

a loud voice, and attended with the outpouring of His Spirit in a large measure. *Testimonies to Ministers*, page 91.

As we behold the Lamb of God as the great divine "By Whom" channel of the Father's blessing, as we build on the divine Cornerstone who inherited all things of the Father, as our families, communities and churches discern the beauty of Christ as the only begotten of the Father and begin to pattern ourselves after Father and Son, then the earth will be lightened with the glory of Christ.

Is it not the revelation of Christ as the Cornerstone of every aspect of our society that is the key to revival and reformation, thus forming a joyous, organised body that is focused and eager to share what has brought them so much joy?

We are told concerning the outpouring of the Spirit at the time of Pentecost:

> **Acts 2:1** And when the day of Pentecost was fully come, they were all with one accord in one place.

How do people come into one accord without a divine pattern for how we should relate to one another? Those who imagine that the Holy Spirit will simply cause us to be in harmony with each other without an understanding of Heaven's divine order as revealed in the Father and His Son will wait in vain for unity to come. Does it not make sense that the Spirit of God will open with great power when each section of the channel of blessing patterns itself after the great original "Of Whom" and "By Whom"?

Notice how this angel in Rev 18:1 comes down with great power or authority. We know that all authority comes from God and therefore this message will come with power upon those who learn to recognise God's authority structure. We know that all authority has already been given to Christ.

> **Matt 28:18** And Jesus came and spake unto them, saying, All power is given unto me in heaven and in earth.

Is the ability of Christ to dispense rich gifts and delegate His authority dependent upon God's people accepting the testimony of God concerning His Son, meaning that they believe that Jesus is His Son? Then as we step into the "Of Whom" and "By Whom" pattern, we are fully ready to receive the power that was given to Christ by His Father.

Can we see that in reverencing the Son of God and coming under His shadow, we begin to see the great authority that He has, and we can be blessed and protected by it?

Friends, I present to you the chief Cornerstone of our faith – The Lord Jesus Christ, the Son of the Father in truth and love. 2 John 1:3.

This revelation of Christ as related to His Father, exposes the work of Babylon and her efforts to replace the Cornerstone. I have presented to you how I see that Adventism has repeated the work of Samson and the sons of Eli to lead us into captivity. Yet deliverance is at hand.

Let us take up the work of repentance, prayer and pleading for our leaders in whatever station they occupy. Let us appeal and submit ourselves to our church leaders that Christ might be placed before them in a spirit of meekness and fear.

I trust that soon our Father will indeed answer the prayer of His Son:

> **John 17:1-3** These words spake Jesus, and lifted up his eyes to heaven, and said, Father, the hour is come; glorify thy Son, that thy Son also may glorify thee: (2) As thou hast given him power over all flesh, that he should give eternal life to as many as thou hast given him. (3) And this is life eternal, that they might know thee the only true God, and Jesus Christ, whom thou hast sent.

Appendix A

Statement of Relevant Fundamental Principles in the 1914 SDA Yearbook

Seventh-day Adventists have no creed but the Bible; but they hold to certain well-defined points of faith, for which they feel prepared to give a reason "to every man that asketh" them. **The following propositions may be taken as a summary of the principal features of their religious faith, upon which there is, so far as is known, entire unanimity throughout the body.** They believe: —

1. That there is one God, a personal, spiritual being, the Creator of all things, omnipotent, omniscient, and eternal; infinite in wisdom, holiness, justice, goodness, truth, and mercy; unchangeable, and every where present by his representative, the Holy Spirit. Ps. 139: 7.

2. That there is one Lord Jesus Christ, the Son of the Eternal Father, the one by whom he created all things, and by whom they do consist; that he took on him the nature of the seed of Abraham for the redemption of our fallen race; that he dwelt among men, full of grace and truth, lived our example, died our sacrifice, was raised for our justification, ascended on high to be our only mediator in the sanctuary in heaven, where through the merits of his shed blood, he secures the pardon and forgiveness of the sins of all those who persistently come to him; and as the closing portion of his work as priest, before he takes his throne as king, he will make the great atonement for the sins of all such, and their sins will then be blotted out (Acts 3: 19) and borne away from the sanctuary, as shown in the service of the Levitical priesthood, which foreshadowed and prefigured the ministry of our Lord in heaven. See Leviticus 16; Heb. 8: 4, 5; 9: 6, 7.

3. That the Holy Scriptures of the Old and New Testaments were given by inspiration of God, contain a full revelation of his will to man, and are the only infallible rule of faith and practise.

Appendix B

Relevant Baptismal Vow
from the 1986 SDA Church Manual

Baptismal Vow. —In the presence of the church or in the presence of a properly appointed body (see p. 43), the following questions should be posed and answered in the affirmative by candidates for baptism, and by those being received on profession of faith.

1. Do you believe in God the Father, in His Son Jesus Christ, and in the Holy Spirit?

Relevant Baptismal Vow
from the 1990 SDA Church Manual

Baptismal Vow.—Candidates for baptism or those being received into fellowship by profession of faith shall affirm their acceptance of the following doctrinal beliefs of the Seventh-day Adventist Church in the presence of the church or other properly appointed body (see page 43). The minister or elder should address the questions to the candidate(s), whose reply may be by verbal assent or by raising the hand.

Commitment

1. Do you believe there is one God: Father, Son, and Holy Spirit, a unity of three coeternal Persons?

The 1986 baptismal vow expresses God as Father and that He has a Son. The use of the word "His" is possessive. It also asks for a belief in the Holy Spirit which is correct.

The 1990 statement expresses one God in three persons without the possessive "His" between Father and Son. The understanding of Co-eternal is three self-originating powers without the Son coming forth or being begotten from the Father. This is a very different god that the candidate is vowing to serve. The term "Son" is a title of His work or office rather than an expression of who He actually is.

If you were baptised before 1990, then you are still faithful to your baptismal vow in rejecting the three person, one God, Trinity.

We invite you to view the complete
selection of titles we publish at:

www.AspectBooks.com

Scan with your mobile
device to go directly
to our website.

Please write or email us your praises, reactions, or
thoughts about this or any other book we publish at:

ASPECT Books

www.ASPECTBooks.com

P.O. Box 954
Ringgold, GA 30736

info@AspectBooks.com

Aspect Books titles may be purchased in bulk for
educational, business, fund-raising, or sales promotional use.
For information, please e-mail

BulkSales@AspectBooks.com

Finally, if you are interested in seeing
your own book in print, please contact us at

publishing@AspectBooks.com

We would be happy to review your manuscript for free.

www.ingramcontent.com/pod-product-compliance
Lightning Source LLC
Chambersburg PA
CBHW070817100426
42742CB00012B/2379